# The CAPE TOWN
# COMMITMENT
## Study Edition

D1600177

# *The* CAPE TOWN
# COMMITMENT
## *Study Edition*

*A Confession of Faith and a Call to Action*

# ROSE DOWSETT

**The Cape Town Commitment: Study Edition**

Hendrickson Publishers Marketing, LLC
P. O. Box 3473
Peabody, Massachusetts 01961-3473

ISBN 978-1-61970-027-7

Printed in the United States of America

First Hendrickson Edition Printing — October 2012

**Library of Congress Cataloging-in-Publication Data**
A catalog record for this book is available from the Library of Congress
Hendrickson Publishers Marketing, LLC  ISBN 978-1-61970-027-7

# Contents

Part II: For the World We Serve: The Cape Town Call to Action

# Publisher's Preface to the Study Edition

The importance of *The Cape Town Commitment* must not be underestimated. As Doug Birdsall states in his Foreword, it offers a blueprint for the future endeavour of The Lausanne Movement and we trust it will affect individuals, churches, and institutions in their outreach to the whole world. For this reason we have published this edition with questions for reflection, and with additional biblical references for study. It offers guidance to all who seek to understand its opening "The Cape Town Confession of Faith" more deeply, and to find their place in the outworking of "The Cape Town Call to Action," which has been adopted by leaders of the church in 198 nations.

Additional material from Congress discussions is included in Section II of this expanded Study Edition. This material is presented with the subhead

*in a shaded line*

and the text in a lighter, greyed font.

A 112-page annotated bibliography for further study of *The Cape Town Commitment* is available online at www.lausanne.org. While the bibliography is designed primarily for those teaching *The Cape Town Commitment* at the graduate school and seminary level, it will also be useful for church or workplace fellowships seeking to deepen their grasp of its content.

# Using the Study Edition

*The Cape Town Commitment* (CTC) is not Scripture, and it must sit under Scripture's searching authority. We do not wish to make too-large claims for the CTC. Because it is a human creation, it will be flawed and incomplete. At the same time, those who wrote it worked hard and prayerfully to try to ensure that everything in it flows from and is in tune with Scripture. For the CTC to be meaningful and useful, Christians need to study it carefully, measuring it against God's Word, and then prayerfully think about how to translate it into action.

## Why a study guide?

With any long document, it is helpful to break it down into sections for closer study and reflection. This study guide is designed to help us to do that.

Each part of the CTC is incomplete without the other. Part I, "The Cape Town Confession of Faith," establishes a theological framework for Christian discipleship and for mission. Part II, "The Cape Town Call to Action," focuses on the central themes of the Congress, and on what we need to do. Theology without action degenerates swiftly into philosophy; action without theology degenerates swiftly into activism and humanism. Theology and action must be kept together, each informing the other.

Studying small sections at a time will help us engage more deeply with the text. It will also be especially helpful where the *Cape Town Commitment* is studied in local congregations, seminary classes, or in small groups.

# Different ways of studying

One of the difficulties in writing a study guide is that in different cultures and contexts people have widely varying ways of processing information—studying it, organising it, sharing it in a group, and responding to it. For instance:

Some of us are accustomed to analyse logically and in linear fashion. We may be comfortable with the written word. We may like sitting with pen in hand and writing answers in spaces provided, or doing the same thing on a computer.

Some of us may be happy studying on our own in a quiet place and with ample time for reflection.

Some of us prefer to work in groups, and learn orally. Here, study and decisions on action become a community task just like every other part of life.

Some of us express everything that is important to us in song and transmit it in this form through the community and down the generations. From the days of the Psalms onwards, this has been central to internalising God's truth and feeding faith.

Some of us find it difficult to engage with ideas and propositions and need to learn through stories and concrete illustrations. The Bible is full of them!

Some of us expect "an expert" or our leader to tell us what to think and do and would regard it as unacceptable to voice our opinions until we are very senior or have heard what our leader thinks.

Some of us find emotional engagement or practical action more compelling than intellectual engagement.

Some of us are big-picture people and find close, detailed examination of a small part of the whole difficult. Others of us prefer to handle information in small chunks.

Adapt this study edition to suit your context and your preferred ways of learning. The questions are designed for you to dig deeper, on your own or in group discussion, and to form a prayerful response and realistic action.

## Diversity in our unity . . . and unity in our diversity

The church is global as never before: praise God! But as God's Word has taken root in different cultures and languages, the church has become increasingly complex in the way in which different communities contextualise the faith. Today's constituencies for The Lausanne Movement and the World Evangelical Alliance (WEA) have become diverse in a way unimaginable a few decades ago.

Some find this unsettling and would like to impose one template of orthodoxy and orthopraxis—that is, formulations of theology and formulations of practice—on everyone everywhere. Others rejoice in the diversity. The CTC is not a template of orthodoxy and does not make claims to be. It does, however, draw together many different Christian streams, as we unite around God's gospel and Word and around a shared commitment to "make disciples of all nations," all in the context of worship of the triune God. Our prayer is for breadth within boundaries—boundaries set by God's Word.

Because of the careful, extensive process by which the CTC was drawn up, we dare to believe that it is worthy of close study, that it may in the grace of God be an instrument of greater unity among God's people, and that it may in some measure provide an agreed roadmap as we work together to take the good news of Jesus Christ to the nations.

So, we invite you to join us on this journey, for the glory of God and the good of his precious world. As you study, whether on your own or in a group or congregation, first read (or hear) the section to which the questions relate. In particular, make sure you look at the Scripture references, because these are our true foundation. In each section, there are overview questions, especially helpful for those who need just one concept to ponder. Then there are further questions for those who wish and are able to dig deeper.

*Rose Dowsett*
*Glasgow, Scotland*

# FOREWORD

The Third Lausanne Congress on World Evangelization (Cape Town, 16–25 October 2010) brought together 4,200 evangelical leaders from 198 countries, and extended to hundreds of thousands more, participating in meetings around the world, and online. Its goal? To bring a fresh challenge to the global Church to bear witness to Jesus Christ and all his teaching—in every nation, in every sphere of society, and in the realm of ideas.

*The Cape Town Commitment* is the fruit of this endeavour. It stands in an historic line, building on both *The Lausanne Covenant* and *The Manila Manifesto*. It is in two parts. Part I sets out biblical convictions, passed down to us in the Scriptures, and Part II sounds the call to action.

How was Part I shaped? It was first discussed in Minneapolis in December 2009, at a gathering of 18 invited theologians and evangelical leaders, drawn from all continents. A smaller group, led by Dr. Christopher J. H. Wright, chair of the Lausanne Theology Working Group, was asked to prepare a final document, ready to be presented to the Congress.

How was Part II shaped? An extensive listening process began more than three years before the Congress. The Lausanne Movement's International Deputy Directors each arranged consultations in their regions, where Christian leaders were asked to identify major challenges facing the Church. Six key issues emerged. These (1) defined the Congress programme and (2) formed the framework for the call to action. This listening process continued on through the Congress, as Chris Wright and the Statement Working Group worked to record all contributions faithfully. It was a herculean and monumental effort.

*The Cape Town Commitment* will now act as a blueprint for The Lausanne Movement over the next ten years. Its prophetic call to work and to pray will, we hope, draw churches, mission agencies, seminaries, Christians in the workplace, and student fellowships on campus to embrace it and to find their part in its outworking.

Many doctrinal statements affirm what the Church believes. We wished to go further and to link belief with praxis. Our model was that of the Apostle Paul, whose theological teaching was fleshed out in practical instruction. For example, in Colossians his profound and wonderful portrayal of the supremacy of Christ issues in down-to-earth teaching on what it means to be rooted in Christ.

We distinguish what is at the heart of the Christian gospel, i.e., primary truths on which we must have unity, from secondary issues, where sincere Christians disagree in their interpretation of what the Bible teaches or requires. We have worked here to model Lausanne's principle of "breadth within boundaries," and in Part I those boundaries are clearly defined.

All through this process we were delighted to collaborate with the World Evangelical Alliance (WEA) who partnered with us in each stage. The leaders of the WEA are in full agreement with both "The Cape Town Confession of Faith" and "The Cape Town Call to Action."

While we speak and write from the evangelical tradition in The Lausanne Movement, we affirm the oneness of the Body of Christ and gladly recognize that there are many followers of the Lord Jesus Christ within other traditions. We welcomed senior representatives from several historic churches of other traditions as observers in Cape Town, and we trust *The Cape Town Commitment* may be helpful to churches of all traditions. We offer it in a humble spirit.

What are our hopes for *The Cape Town Commitment*? We trust that it will be talked about, discussed, and afforded weight as a united statement from evangelicals globally; that it will shape agendas in Christian ministry; that it will strengthen thought-leaders in the public arena; and that bold initiatives and partnerships will issue from it.

May the Word of God light our path, and may the grace of the Lord Jesus Christ, and the love of God, and the fellowship of the Holy Spirit be with each one of us.

*S. Douglas Birdsall*
*Executive Chairman*

*Lindsay Brown*
*International Director*

# PREAMBLE

*As members of the worldwide Church of Jesus Christ, we joyfully affirm our commitment to the living God and his saving purposes through the Lord Jesus Christ. For his sake we renew our commitment to the vision and goals of The Lausanne Movement.*

This means two things:

*First*, we remain committed to the task of bearing worldwide witness to Jesus Christ and all his teaching. The First Lausanne Congress (1974) was convened for the task of world evangelization. Among its major gifts to the world Church were: (1) *The Lausanne Covenant*; (2) a new awareness of the number of unreached people groups; and (3) a fresh discovery of the holistic nature of the biblical gospel and of Christian mission. The Second Lausanne Congress, in Manila (1989), gave birth to more than 300 strategic partnerships in world evangelization, including many that involved co-operation between nations in all parts of the globe.

And *second*, we remain committed to the primary documents of the Movement—*The Lausanne Covenant* (1974), and *The Manila Manifesto* (1989). These documents clearly express core truths of the biblical gospel and apply them to our practical mission in ways that are still relevant and challenging. We confess that we have not been faithful to commitments made in those documents. But we commend them and stand by them, as we seek to discern how we must express and apply the eternal truth of the gospel in the ever-changing world of our own generation.[1]

---

[1] See www.lausanne.org. *The Lausanne Covenant*, complete text with a study guide by John Stott, is available in the Didasko Files series.

## The realities of change

Almost everything about the way we live, think, and relate to one another is changing at an accelerating pace. For good or ill, we feel the impact of globalization, of the digital revolution, and of the changing balance of economic and political power in the world. Some things we face cause us grief and anxiety—global poverty, war, ethnic conflict, disease, the ecological crisis and climate change. But one great change in our world is a cause for rejoicing—and that is the growth of the global Church of Christ.

The fact that the Third Lausanne Congress took place in Africa is proof of this. At least two thirds of all the world's Christians now live in the continents of the global south and east. The composition of our Cape Town Congress reflected this enormous shift in world Christianity in the century since the Edinburgh Missionary Conference in 1910. We rejoice in the amazing growth of the Church in Africa, and we rejoice that our African sisters and brothers in Christ hosted this Congress. At the same time, we could not meet in South Africa without being mindful of the past years of suffering under apartheid. So we give thanks for the progress of the gospel and the sovereign righteousness of God at work in recent history, while wrestling still with the ongoing legacy of evil and injustice. Such is the double witness and role of the Church in every place.

We must respond in Christian mission to the realities of our own generation. We must also learn from that mixture of wisdom and error, of achievement and failure, that we inherit from previous generations. We honour and lament the past, and we engage with the future, in the name of the God who holds all history in his hand.

## Unchanged realities

In a world which works to re-invent itself at an ever-accelerated pace, some things remain the same. These great truths provide the biblical rationale for our missional engagement.

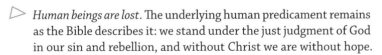 *Human beings are lost.* The underlying human predicament remains as the Bible describes it: we stand under the just judgment of God in our sin and rebellion, and without Christ we are without hope.

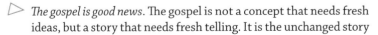 *The gospel is good news.* The gospel is not a concept that needs fresh ideas, but a story that needs fresh telling. It is the unchanged story

of what God has done to save the world, supremely in the historical events of the life, death, resurrection, and reign of Jesus Christ. In Christ there is hope.

▷ *The Church's mission goes on.* The mission of God continues to the ends of the earth and to the end of the world. The day will come when the kingdoms of the world will become the kingdom of our God and of his Christ and God will dwell with his redeemed humanity in the new creation. Until that day, the Church's participation in God's mission continues, in joyful urgency, and with fresh and exciting opportunities in every generation including our own.

## The passion of our love

This Statement is framed in the language of love. Love is the language of covenant. The biblical covenants, old and new, are the expression of God's redeeming love and grace reaching out to lost humanity and spoiled creation. They call for our love in return. Our love shows itself in trust, obedience, and passionate commitment to our covenant Lord. *The Lausanne Covenant* defined evangelization as "*the whole Church taking the whole gospel to the whole world.*" That is still our passion. So we renew that covenant by affirming again:

▷ *Our love for the whole gospel*, as God's glorious good news in Christ, for every dimension of his creation, for it has all been ravaged by sin and evil;

▷ *Our love for the whole Church*, as God's people, redeemed by Christ from every nation on earth and every age of history, to share God's mission in this age and glorify him for ever in the age to come;

▷ *Our love for the whole world*, so far from God but so close to his heart, the world that God so loved that he gave his only Son for its salvation.

In the grip of that three-fold love, we commit ourselves afresh to be the whole Church, to believe, obey, and share the whole gospel, and to go to the whole world to make disciples of all nations.

## Overview questions

1. The realities of change: In your context, what are the changes over the last ten or twenty years which are most affecting your society, God's people, and you personally? Which changes affect each of these for good, and which for harm? Why? How could you respond differently to them to bring greater glory to God?

## Digging deeper

2. Unchanged realities: Taking in turn "human beings are lost," "the gospel is good news," and "the Church's mission goes on," put into your own words what each means. Which Scriptures would you turn to? In your culture, what are the main obstacles to people believing these big truths?

3. Using a resource such as *Operation World* (http://www.operationworld. org/a-countries) identify three countries or people groups where the church has grown significantly larger during the past few decades, and three where the church has become smaller in the same period. With the help of the material given, spend some time praying for each of these countries and for the witness of the Lord's people there.

4. The passion of our love: What does the Bible mean by "covenant"? How is "love" the language of biblical covenant? How does this differ from contemporary ideas about "love" in your culture and context? All love needs to be nurtured, or it withers away. How do we nurture love for God, so that it remains fresh and growing?

# Part I

## FOR THE LORD WE LOVE: THE CAPE TOWN CONFESSION OF FAITH

# 1

# WE LOVE BECAUSE GOD FIRST LOVED US

*The mission of God flows from the love of God. The mission of God's people flows from our love for God and for all that God loves. World evangelization is the outflow of God's love to us and through us. We affirm the primacy of God's grace and we then respond to that grace by faith, demonstrated through the obedience of love. We love because God first loved us and sent his Son to be the propitiation for our sins.*[2]

A. *Love for God and love for neighbour constitute the first and greatest commandments on which hang all the law and the prophets.* Love is the fulfilling of the law, and the first named fruit of the Spirit. Love is the evidence that we are born again; the assurance that we know God; and the proof that God dwells within us. Love is the new commandment of Christ, who told his disciples that only as they obeyed this commandment would their mission be visible and believable. Christian love for one another is how the unseen God, who made himself visible through his incarnate Son, goes on making himself visible to the world. Love was among the first things that Paul observed and commended among new believers, along with faith and hope. But love is the greatest, for love never ends.[3]

B. *Such love is not weak or sentimental.* The love of God is covenantally faithful, committed, self-giving, sacrificial, strong, and holy. Since God is love, love permeates God's whole being and all his actions, his justice as well as his compassion. God's love extends over all his creation. We are commanded to love in ways that reflect the love of God in all those same dimensions. That is what it means to walk in the way of the Lord.[4]

---

[2] Galatians 5:6; John 14:21; 1 John 4:9, 19.
[3] Matthew 22:37–40; Romans 13:8–10; Galatians 5:22; 1 Peter 1:22; 1 John 3:14; 4:7–21; John 13:34–35; John 1:18 & 1 John 4:12; 1 Thessalonians 1:3; 1 Corinthians 13:8, 13.
[4] Deuteronomy 7:7–9; Hosea 2:19–20; 11:1; Psalms 103; 145:9, 13, 17; Galatians 2:20; Deuteronomy 10:12–19.

C. *So in framing our convictions and our commitments in terms of love, we are taking up the most basic and demanding biblical challenge of all:*

1. to love the Lord our God with all our heart and soul and mind and strength;

2. to love our neighbour (including the foreigner and the enemy) as ourselves;

3. to love one another as God in Christ has loved us, and

4. to love the world with the love of the One who gave his only Son that the world through him might be saved.[5]

D. *Such love is the gift of God poured out in our hearts, but it is also the command of God requiring the obedience of our wills.* Such love means to be like Christ himself: robust in endurance, yet gentle in humility; tough in resisting evil, yet tender in compassion for the suffering; courageous in suffering and faithful even unto death. Such love was modelled by Christ on earth and is measured by the risen Christ in glory.[6]

*We affirm that such comprehensive biblical love should be the defining identity and hallmark of disciples of Jesus. In response to the prayer and command of Jesus, we long that it should be so for us. Sadly we confess that too often it is not. So we re-commit ourselves afresh to make every effort to live, think, speak, and behave in ways that express what it means to walk in love—love for God, love for one another and love for the world.*

## Overview questions

1. Read John 3:16–17 and 1 John 4:7–21. What do these passages teach us about the love of God for us and the way in which we are to respond? Why is it so important to understand that "we love because God first loved us" rather than that "God loves us because we first loved him"?

---

[5] Deuteronomy 6:4–5; Matthew 22:37; Leviticus 19:18, 34; Matthew 5:43–45; John 15:12; Ephesians 4:32; John 3:16–17.
[6] Romans 5:5; 2 Corinthians 5:14; Revelation 2:4.

**Digging deeper**

2. Jesus taught, "Love the Lord your God with all your heart and with all your soul and with all your mind. This is the first and greatest commandment" (Matthew 22:37–38). What does this mean in everyday life today? What effect will it have on our beliefs, values, actions, and relationships? What changes may we need to make in our discipleship?

3. Jesus went on to say, "And the second is like it: 'Love your neighbour as yourself.' All the Law and Prophets hang on these two commandments" (Matthew 22:39–40). Who is your neighbour? What does love for our neighbour look like in everyday life? What does it mean that "all the Law and Prophets hang on these two commandments"? How will that affect how we read the Old Testament? Give some examples.

4. How would you explain the love of God to a non-Christian? Some people's experiences make it hard for them to believe that God loves them, and to receive his love as a reality in their lives. Why do you think that is? How would you help such a person?

5. Compose a prayer or a hymn thanking God for his love.

6. With a group of Christian friends, or in your family, pray together for neighbours and work colleagues, asking that you may recognise opportunities to show and explain the love of God to them. Share testimonies of times when you have already experienced God "opening up the way" for witness. Pray for believers who are persecuted, that they may be able to love their enemies rather than retaliate with harm to them.

# 2

# WE LOVE THE LIVING GOD

*Our God whom we love reveals himself in the Bible as the one, eternal, living God who governs all things according to his sovereign will and for his saving purpose. In the unity of Father, Son, and Holy Spirit, God alone is the Creator, Ruler, Judge, and Saviour of the world.[7] So we love God—thanking him for our place in creation, submitting to his sovereign providence, trusting in his justice, and praising him for the salvation he has accomplished for us.*

A. *We love God above all rivals.* We are commanded to love and worship the living God alone. But like Old Testament Israel we allow our love for God to be adulterated by going after the gods of this world, the gods of the people around us.[8] We fall into syncretism, enticed by many idols such as greed, power, and success, serving mammon rather than God. We accept dominant political and economic ideologies without biblical critique. We are tempted to compromise our belief in the uniqueness of Christ under the pressure of religious pluralism. Like Israel we need to hear the call of the prophets and of Jesus himself to repent, to forsake all such rivals, and to return to obedient love and worship of God alone.

B. *We love God with passion for his glory.* The greatest motivation for our mission is the same as that which drives the mission of God himself— that the one true living God should be known and glorified throughout his whole creation. That is God's ultimate goal and should be our greatest joy.

If God desires every knee to bow to Jesus and every tongue to confess him, so should we. We should be "jealous" (as Scripture sometimes puts it) for the

---

[7] Deuteronomy 4:35, 39; Psalm 33:6–9; Jeremiah 10:10–12; Deuteronomy 10:14; Isaiah 40:22–24; Psalm 33:10–11, 13–15; Psalm 96:10–13; Psalm 36:6; Isaiah 45:22.

[8] Deuteronomy 4 and 6.

honour of his name—troubled when it remains unknown, hurt when it is ignored, indignant when it is blasphemed, and all the time anxious and determined that it shall be given the honour and glory which are due to it. The highest of all missionary motives is neither obedience to the Great Commission (important as that is), nor love for sinners who are alienated and perishing (strong as that incentive is, especially when we contemplate the wrath of God) but rather zeal—burning and passionate zeal—for the glory of Jesus Christ. . . . Before this supreme goal of the Christian mission, all unworthy motives wither and die.[9]

It should be our greatest grief that in our world the living God is not glorified. The living God is denied in aggressive atheism. The one true God is replaced or distorted in the practice of world religions. Our Lord Jesus Christ is abused and misrepresented in some popular cultures. And the face of the God of biblical revelation is obscured by Christian nominalism, syncretism, and hypocrisy.

*Loving God in the midst of a world that rejects or distorts him, calls for bold but humble witness to our God; robust but gracious defence of the truth of the gospel of Christ, God's Son; and prayerful trust in the convicting and convincing work of his Holy Spirit. We commit ourselves to such witness, for if we claim to love God we must share God's greatest priority, which is that his name and his Word should be exalted above all things.*[10]

## Overview questions

1. What does it mean to say that "God is alive"? How would you explain that to an unbeliever or to a child? "We love God with a passion for his glory"; "It should be our greatest grief that in our world the living God is not glorified." If we truly believe this, and that God is alive, how would it show in our personal lives, our church life, and our agency life? What changes do we need to make?

---

[9] John Stott, *The Message of Romans,* The Bible Speaks Today (Leicester: Inter-Varsity Press, 1994), 53.
[10] Psalm 138:2.

**Digging deeper**

2. What are some of the "gods of this world" that influence you in your context? What are the gods that shape your culture? In this setting, what would be the concrete evidence of repentance? How can we live distinctively as Christians without withdrawing from our society?

3. Read Exodus 20:1–4. How must we live to obey the command to "have no other gods before me"? What does God mean when he says (Exodus 20:5) that he is a "jealous God"? How would you explain that to an unbeliever? How must we live to demonstrate it to an unbeliever?

4. In the group which is studying the CTC with you, share testimonies relating to your present experience of God being alive. Then pray for one another to have the courage to testify, naturally and graciously, to unbelievers you will encounter in the week ahead.

5. Write an article, or prepare a presentation, to interact with today's aggressive "new atheism." Relate it to a specific audience—for instance, a student group. If the "new atheism" is not yet an issue in your community, write the article or prepare the presentation to show how you would introduce the living God in your religious and philosophical context.

# 3

# We Love God the Father

*Through Jesus Christ, God's Son—and through him alone as the way, the truth and the life—we come to know and love God as Father. As the Holy Spirit testifies with our spirit that we are God's children, so we cry the words Jesus prayed, "Abba, Father," and we pray the prayer Jesus taught, "Our Father." Our love for Jesus, proved by obeying him, is met by the Father's love for us as the Father and the Son make their home in us, in mutual giving and receiving of love.*[11] *This intimate relationship has deep biblical foundations.*

A. *We love God as the Father of his people.* Old Testament Israel knew God as Father, as the one who brought them into existence, carried them and disciplined them, called for their obedience, longed for their love, and exercised compassionate forgiveness and patient enduring love.[12] All these remain true for us as God's people in Christ in our relationship with our Father God.

B. *We love God as the Father, who so loved the world that he gave his only Son for our salvation.* How great the Father's love for us that we should be called the children of God. How immeasurable the love of the Father who did not spare his only Son, but gave him up for us all. This love of the Father in giving the Son was mirrored by the self-giving love of the Son. There was complete harmony of will in the work of atonement that the Father and the Son accomplished at the cross, through the eternal Spirit. The Father loved the world and gave his Son; "the Son of God loved me and gave himself for me." This unity of Father and Son, affirmed by Jesus himself, is echoed in Paul's most repeated greeting of "grace and peace from God our Father and the Lord Jesus Christ, who gave himself for our sins . . . according to the will of our God and Father, to whom be glory for ever and ever. Amen."[13]

---

[11] John 14:6; Romans 8:14–15; Matthew 6:9; John 14:21–23.
[12] Deuteronomy 32:6, 18; 1:31; 8:5; Isaiah 1:2; Malachi 1:6; Jeremiah 3:4, 19; 31:9; Hosea 11:2; Psalm 103:13; Isaiah 63:16; 64:8–9.
[13] John 3:16; 1 John 3:1; Romans 8:32; Hebrews 9:14; Galatians 2:20; Galatians 1:4–5.

*C. We love God as the Father whose character we reflect and whose care we trust.* In the Sermon on the Mount Jesus repeatedly points to our heavenly Father as the model or focus for our action. We are to be peacemakers, as sons of God. We are to do good deeds, so that our Father receives the praise. We are to love our enemies in reflection of God's Fatherly love. We are to practise our giving, praying, and fasting for our Father's eyes only. We are to forgive others as our Father forgives us. We are to have no anxiety but trust in our Father's provision. With such behaviour flowing from Christian character, we do the will of our Father in heaven, within the kingdom of God.[14]

*We confess that we have often neglected the truth of the Fatherhood of God and deprived ourselves of the riches of our relationship with him. We commit ourselves afresh to come to the Father through Jesus the Son: to receive and respond to his Fatherly love; to live in obedience under his Fatherly discipline; to reflect his Fatherly character in all our behaviour and attitudes; and to trust in his Fatherly provision in whatever circumstances he leads us.*

## Overview questions

1. In the Sermon on the Mount, Matthew repeatedly quotes Jesus as saying "your Father in heaven," "your heavenly Father." Look up Matthew 5:16, 45, 48; 6:1, 4, 6, 8–9, 14–15, 18, 26, 32; 7:11. What do you learn about the Fatherhood of God? How are we to imitate him? How shall we express love for God the Father in our daily lives?

## Digging deeper

2. Why would Jesus' contemporaries have been surprised and perhaps shocked to hear him speaking of God as our Father, and his Father, in loving and intimate terms? How would people of other faiths react to this revelation of God?

---

[14] Matthew 5:9, 16, 43–48; 6:4, 6, 14–15, 18, 25–32; 7:21–23.

3. How does the Bible describe the relationship between God the Father and the Lord Jesus Christ, and between Father and Son and Holy Spirit? Which passages would you turn to in order to demonstrate the mystery of Father, Son, and Spirit, each being fully God, yet one?

4. Why is it important to affirm that Father, Son, and Spirit were all fully and voluntarily involved in our salvation through Christ's atoning death on the cross and his resurrection? Look at John 3:16; Matthew 20:28; Luke 23:46; Acts 2:31–33, 36; Romans 8:32; and Galatians 1:3–5. Pause and give thanks to God.

5. Some people have suffered at the hands of their earthly fathers and find it hard to approach God as their heavenly Father. How might you show them that God is good, loving, and absolutely dependable? In what practical ways should a church family care for those who have been damaged by their earthly parents, or abandoned, or orphaned?

# 4

# WE LOVE GOD THE SON

*God commanded Israel to love the LORD God with exclusive loyalty. Likewise for us, loving the Lord Jesus Christ means that we steadfastly affirm that he alone is Saviour, Lord, and God. The Bible teaches that Jesus performs the same sovereign actions as God alone. Christ is Creator of the universe, Ruler of history, Judge of all nations, and Saviour of all who turn to God.[15] He shares the identity of God in the divine equality and unity of Father, Son, and Holy Spirit. Just as God called Israel to love him in covenantal faith, obedience, and servant-witness, we affirm our love for Jesus Christ by trusting in him, obeying him, and making him known.*

A. *We trust in Christ.* We believe the testimony of the Gospels that Jesus of Nazareth is the Messiah, the one appointed and sent by God to fulfil the unique mission of Old Testament Israel, that is to bring the blessing of God's salvation to all nations, as God promised to Abraham.

1. A. In Jesus, conceived by the Holy Spirit and born of the Virgin Mary, God took our human flesh and lived among us, fully God and fully human.

2. In his life Jesus walked in perfect faithfulness and obedience to God. He announced and taught the kingdom of God, and modelled the way his disciples must live under God's reign.

3. In his ministry and miracles, Jesus announced and demonstrated the victory of the kingdom of God over evil and evil powers.

---

[15] John 1:3; 1 Corinthians 8:4–6; Hebrews 1:2; Colossians 1:15–17; Psalm 110:1; Mark 14:61–64; Ephesians 1:20–23; Revelation 1:5; 3:14; 5:9–10; Romans 2:16; 2 Thessalonians 1:5–10; 2 Corinthians 5:10; Romans 14:9–12; Matthew 1:21; Luke 2:30; Acts 4:12; 15:11; Romans 10:9; Titus 2:13; Hebrews 2:10; 5:9; 7:25; Revelation 7:10.

4. In his death on the cross, Jesus took our sin upon himself in our place, bearing its full cost, penalty, and shame, defeated death and the powers of evil, and accomplished the reconciliation and redemption of all creation.

5. In his bodily resurrection, Jesus was vindicated and exalted by God, completed and demonstrated the full victory of the cross, and became the forerunner of redeemed humanity and restored creation.

6. Since his ascension, Jesus is reigning as Lord over all history and creation.

7. At his return, Jesus will execute God's judgment, destroy Satan, evil, and death, and establish the universal reign of God.

B. *We obey Christ.* Jesus calls us to discipleship, to take up our cross and follow him in the path of self-denial, servanthood, and obedience. "If you love me, keep my commandments," he said. "Why do you call me Lord, Lord, and do not do the things I say?" We are called to live as Christ lived and to love as Christ loved. To profess Christ while ignoring his commands is dangerous folly. Jesus warns us that many who claim his name with spectacular and miraculous ministries will find themselves disowned by him as evildoers.[16] We take heed to Christ's warning, for none of us is immune to such fearful danger.

C. *We proclaim Christ.* In Christ alone God has fully and finally revealed himself, and through Christ alone God has achieved salvation for the world. We therefore kneel as disciples at the feet of Jesus of Nazareth and say to him with Peter, "You are the Christ, the Son of the Living God," and with Thomas, "My Lord and my God." Though we have not seen him, we love him. And we rejoice with hope as we long for the day of his return when we shall see him as he is. Until that day we join Peter and John in proclaiming that "there is salvation in no one else, for there is no other name under heaven by which we must be saved."[17]

*We commit ourselves afresh to bear witness to Jesus Christ and all his teaching, in all the world, knowing that we can bear such witness only if we are living in obedience to his teaching ourselves.*

---

[16] Luke 6:46; 1 John 2:3–6; Matthew 7:21–23.
[17] Matthew 16:16; John 20:28; 1 Peter 1:8; 1 John 3:1–3; Acts 4:12.

## Overview questions

1. At the very heart of the Christian faith is the *person* of Jesus Christ: not just ideas or propositions, but a real historical *person*. Spend some time re-reading a Gospel, praying that you will have a fresh vision of this precious, unique person. Under (a) of this section's text, there are listed seven key elements of the life and ministry of our Lord Jesus Christ. Taking each one in turn, how should it feed our love for him?

## Digging deeper

2. It is because Jesus Christ is a person that it is meaningful to speak of love for him. How do love for him and trust in him fit together? How can we help one another to grow in love and trust? Give some practical examples.

3. What does it mean "to take up our cross" in practical daily life? Read Matthew 10:37–39 and Luke 9:18–27. What is the context of each of these passages? What would this teaching have meant in its original context? How do we obey it today? What is the cost, and what is the gain? Pause and pray for those for whom obeying this command is very costly in today's world, especially those called upon to endure persecution or even martyrdom.

4. How do we "proclaim Christ" in word, deed, and character in our own context, cross-culturally, and especially in the context of another world religion? Why is it so crucial that the whole world hears about, and sees demonstrated, the "truth as it is in Jesus"? What are the chief obstacles to belief in Jesus in your setting? What are the chief opportunities?

5. Compose a worship song, or create a painting or drama, to express your love for Jesus Christ in response to specific parts of his life and ministry.

# 5

# WE LOVE GOD THE HOLY SPIRIT

*We love the Holy Spirit within the unity of the Trinity, along with God the Father
and God the Son. He is the missionary Spirit sent by the missionary Father and
the missionary Son, breathing life and power into God's missionary Church. We
love and pray for the presence of the Holy Spirit because without the witness of
the Spirit to Christ, our own witness is futile. Without the convicting work
of the Spirit, our preaching is in vain. Without the gifts, guidance, and power of
the Spirit, our mission is mere human effort. And without the fruit of the Spirit,
our unattractive lives cannot reflect the beauty of the gospel.*

*A. In the Old Testament we see the Spirit of God active in creation, in works
of liberation and justice, and in filling and empowering people for every kind of
service.* Spirit-filled prophets looked forward to the coming King and Servant, whose Person and work would be endowed with God's Spirit. Prophets also looked to the coming age that would be marked by the outpouring
of God's Spirit, bringing new life, fresh obedience, and prophetic gifting to
all the people of God, young and old, men and women.[18]

*B. At Pentecost God poured out his Holy Spirit as promised by the prophets
and by Jesus.* The sanctifying Spirit produces his fruit in the lives of believers, and the first fruit is always love. The Spirit fills the Church with his
gifts, which we "eagerly desire" as the indispensable equipment for Christian service. The Spirit gives us power for mission and for the great variety
of works of service. The Spirit enables us to proclaim and demonstrate
the gospel, to discern the truth, to pray effectively, and to prevail over the
forces of darkness. The Spirit inspires and accompanies our worship. The

---

[18] Genesis 1:1–2; Psalm 104:27–30; Job 33:4; Exodus 35:30–36:1; Judges 3:10;
6:34; 13:25; Numbers 11:16–17, 29; Isaiah 63:11–14; 2 Peter 1:20–21; Micah 3:8;
Nehemiah 9:20, 30; Zechariah 7:7–12; Isaiah 11:1–5; 42:1–7; 61:1–3; 32:15–18;
Ezekiel 36:25–27; 37:1–14; Joel 2:28–32.

Spirit strengthens and comforts disciples who are persecuted or on trial for their witness to Christ.[19]

C. *Our engagement in mission, then, is pointless and fruitless without the presence, guidance, and power of the Holy Spirit.* This is true of mission in all its dimensions: evangelism, bearing witness to the truth, discipling, peace-making, social engagement, ethical transformation, caring for creation, overcoming evil powers, casting out demonic spirits, healing the sick, suffering and enduring under persecution. All we do in the name of Christ must be led and empowered by the Holy Spirit. The New Testament makes this clear in the life of the early Church and the teaching of the apostles. It is being demonstrated today in the fruitfulness and growth of Churches where Jesus' followers act confidently in the power of the Holy Spirit, with dependence and expectation.

*There is no true or whole gospel, and no authentic biblical mission, without the Person, work, and power of the Holy Spirit. We pray for a greater awakening to this biblical truth, and for its experience to be reality in all parts of the worldwide body of Christ. However, we are aware of the many abuses that masquerade under the name of the Holy Spirit, the many ways in which all kinds of phenomena are practised and praised which are not the gifts of the Holy Spirit as clearly taught in the New Testament. There is great need for more profound discernment, for clear warnings against delusion, for the exposure of fraudulent and self-serving manipulators who abuse spiritual power for their own ungodly enrichment. Above all there is a great need for sustained biblical teaching and preaching, soaked in humble prayer, that will equip ordinary believers to understand and rejoice in the true gospel and to recognize and reject false gospels.*

## Overview questions

1.  Read Genesis 1:1–2, Isaiah 63:11–14, Numbers 11:16–17, Micah 3:8, and Ezekiel 36:25–27. What do these passages teach us about the activity of the Holy Spirit, long before Pentecost? Is the Holy Spirit still active in the same way today? Find some New Testament references to the Holy Spirit; what do they teach us? Why should we love the Spirit in the same way we are to love the Father and the Son?

---

[19] Acts 2; Galatians 5:22–23; 1 Peter 1:2; Ephesians 4:3–6; 11–12; Romans 12:3–8; 1 Corinthians 12:4–11; 1 Corinthians 14:1; John 20:21–22; 14:16–17, 25–26; 16:12–15; Romans 8:26–27; Ephesians 6:10–18; John 4:23–24; 1 Corinthians 12:3; 14:13–17; Matthew 10:17–20; Luke 21:15.

## Digging deeper

2. "The fruit of the Spirit is love, joy, peace, patience, kindness, goodness, faithfulness, gentleness and self-control" (Galatians 5:22–23). Are these qualities evidenced in your life and in the lives of the Christian communities you know? If not, why not? Give some concrete examples of what difference these fruit make in daily life. How does your culture encourage or discourage these qualities?

3. There are several lists of gifts of the Spirit (e.g., 1 Corinthians 12:1–11, Ephesians 4:11–13). How do we recognise which gifts the Lord has entrusted us with? How do we encourage one another to use the gifts for the glory of God and the good of God's people? How do the different gifts serve the church in its mission? How do we discern when an apparent gift is not truly from the Spirit?

4. In John 3, Nicodemus cannot understand how it is possible to be born again, but Jesus insists that we must be born of the Spirit to enter the kingdom of heaven. How would you explain this to an unbeliever? Why is it especially difficult for Hindus and Buddhists to accept this rebirth? First Peter 1:23–25 links rebirth with "the living and enduring word." How do word, Spirit, and rebirth come together?

5. How is the Holy Spirit active in mission today? In a group, share stories of your own faith journeys and of experiences of the Holy Spirit at work in saving grace in others. How are these stories the same as, or different from, the stories in Acts?

6. Create a celebratory banner related to the ministry of the Holy Spirit, or compose a hymn of praise to all three Persons of the Trinity.

# 6

# WE LOVE GOD'S WORD

*We love God's Word in the Scriptures of the Old and New Testament, echoing the joyful delight of the Psalmist in the Torah, "I love your commands more than gold.... Oh how I love your law." We receive the whole Bible as the Word of God, inspired by God's Spirit, spoken and written through human authors. We submit to it as supremely and uniquely authoritative, governing our belief and our behaviour. We testify to the power of God's Word to accomplish his purpose of salvation. We affirm that the Bible is the final written word of God, not surpassed by any further revelation, but we also rejoice that the Holy Spirit illumines the minds of God's people so that the Bible continues to speak God's truth in fresh ways to people in every culture.*[20]

A. *The Person the Bible reveals.* We love the Bible as a bride loves her husband's letters, not for the paper they are, but for the person who speaks through them. The Bible gives us God's own revelation of his identity, character, purposes, and actions. It is the primary witness to the Lord Jesus Christ. In reading it, we encounter him through his Spirit with great joy. Our love for the Bible is an expression of our love for God.

B. *The story the Bible tells.* The Bible tells the universal story of creation, fall, redemption in history, and new creation. This overarching narrative provides our coherent biblical worldview and shapes our theology. At the centre of this story are the climactic saving events of the cross and resurrection of Christ which constitute the heart of the gospel. It is this story (in the Old and New Testaments) that tells us who we are, what we are here for, and where we are going. This story of God's mission defines our identity, drives our mission, and assures us the ending is in God's hands. This story must shape the memory and hope of God's people and govern the content of their evangelistic witness, as it is passed on from generation to generation. We must make the Bible known by all means possible, for

---

[20] Psalm 119:47, 97; 2 Timothy 3:16–17; 2 Peter 1:21.

its message is for all people on earth. We recommit ourselves, therefore, to the ongoing task of translating, disseminating, and teaching the Scriptures in every culture and language, including those that are predominantly oral or non-literary.

C. *The truth the Bible teaches.* The whole Bible teaches us the whole counsel of God, the truth that God intends us to know. We submit to it as true and trustworthy in all it affirms, for it is the Word of the God who cannot lie and will not fail. It is clear and sufficient in revealing the way of salvation. It is the foundation for exploring and understanding all dimensions of God's truth.

We live, however, in a world full of lies and rejection of the truth. Many cultures display a dominant relativism that denies that any absolute truth exists or can be known. If we love the Bible, then we must rise to the defence of its truth claims. We must find fresh ways to articulate biblical authority in all cultures. We commit ourselves again to strive to defend the truth of God's revelation as part of our labour of love for God's Word.

D. *The life the Bible requires.* "The Word is in your mouth and in your heart so that you may obey it." Jesus and James call us to be doers of the Word and not hearers only.[21] The Bible portrays a quality of life that should mark the believer and the community of believers. From Abraham, through Moses, the Psalmists, prophets and wisdom of Israel, and from Jesus and the apostles, we learn that such a biblical lifestyle includes justice, compassion, humility, integrity, truthfulness, sexual chastity, generosity, kindness, self-denial, hospitality, peace-making, non-retaliation, doing good, forgiveness, joy, contentment, and love—all combined in lives of worship, praise, and faithfulness to God.

*We confess that we easily claim to love the Bible without loving the life it teaches—the life of costly practical obedience to God through Christ. Yet "nothing commends the gospel more eloquently than a transformed life, and nothing brings it into disrepute so much as personal inconsistency. We are charged to behave in a manner that is worthy of the gospel of Christ and even to 'adorn' it, enhancing its beauty by holy lives."[22] For the sake of the gospel of Christ, therefore, we recommit ourselves to prove our love for God's Word by believing and obeying it. There is no biblical mission without biblical living.*

---

[21] Deuteronomy 30:14; Matthew 7:21–27; Luke 6:46; James 1:22–24.
[22] *The Manila Manifesto* Section 7; Titus 2:9–10.

## Overview questions

1. We rightly speak of "the authority of Scripture." What does that mean in everyday life and discipleship? What do we do when our culture, our family, or our workplace conflict with Scripture? How should we respond when another believer understands Scripture differently from us?

## Digging deeper

2. We love God's Word because it is his revelation of himself to us and opens to us his divine intentions for us and the world he has made. In what practical ways can we listen more deeply and more clearly to what he has to say? How can we encourage one another in the Christian community to hear the voice of God and to respond to it?

3. In your group, or with a friend, share testimonies of what you have learned recently from God's Word, and how that is changing your life.

4. In what ways is the story told in the Bible different from the stories told in your culture? How could you share stories from the Bible in your family, your neighbourhood, or your workplace? You yourself are a story: what do unbelievers read and hear when they watch you? Does it match up to the Bible story?

5. In some places, there are many copies of the Bible in circulation but a great famine of the Word of God. Why do you think that is? If it describes your culture, what could you do to change the situation? In some places, Bibles are scarce, so there is a famine of the Word for a different reason. What could you do about it? In some places, as yet only small portions of Scripture have been translated, or even none. What could you do about that? Don't forget to pray as well as discuss, and agree on some practical actions.

# 7

# WE LOVE GOD'S WORLD

*We share God's passion for his world, loving all that God has made, rejoicing in God's providence and justice throughout his creation, proclaiming the good news to all creation and all nations, and longing for the day when the earth will be filled with the knowledge of the glory of God as the waters cover the sea.*[23]

A. *We love the world of God's creation.* This love is not mere sentimental affection for nature (which the Bible nowhere commands), still less is it pantheistic worship of nature (which the Bible expressly forbids). Rather it is the logical outworking of our love for God by caring for what belongs to him. "The earth is the Lord's and everything in it." The earth is the property of the God we claim to love and obey. We care for the earth, most simply, because it belongs to the one whom we call Lord.[24]

The earth is created, sustained, and redeemed by Christ.[25] We cannot claim to love God while abusing what belongs to Christ by right of creation, redemption, and inheritance. We care for the earth and responsibly use its abundant resources, not according to the rationale of the secular world, but for the Lord's sake. If Jesus is Lord of all the earth, we cannot separate our relationship to Christ from how we act in relation to the earth. For to proclaim the gospel that says "Jesus is Lord" is to proclaim the gospel that includes the earth, since Christ's Lordship is over all creation. Creation care is a thus a gospel issue within the Lordship of Christ.

Such love for God's creation demands that we repent of our part in the destruction, waste, and pollution of the earth's resources and our collusion in the toxic idolatry of consumerism. Instead, we commit ourselves

---

[23] Psalm 145:9, 13, 17; Psalm 104:27–30; Psalm 50:6; Mark 16:15; Colossians 1:23; Matthew 28:17–20; Habakkuk 2:14.
[24] Psalm 24:1; Deuteronomy 10:14.
[25] Colossians 1:15–20; Hebrews 1:2–3.

to urgent and prophetic ecological responsibility. We support Christians whose particular missional calling is to environmental advocacy and action, as well as those committed to godly fulfilment of the mandate to provide for human welfare and needs by exercising responsible dominion and stewardship. The Bible declares God's redemptive purpose for creation itself. Integral mission means discerning, proclaiming, and living out, the biblical truth that the gospel is God's good news, through the cross and resurrection of Jesus Christ, for individual persons, and for society, and for creation. All three are broken and suffering because of sin; all three are included in the redeeming love and mission of God; all three must be part of the comprehensive mission of God's people.

B. *We love the world of nations and cultures.* "From one man, God made all nations of humanity, to live on the whole face of the earth." Ethnic diversity is the gift of God in creation and will be preserved in the new creation, when it will be liberated from our fallen divisions and rivalry. Our love for all peoples reflects God's promise to bless all nations on earth and God's mission to create for himself a people drawn from every tribe, language, nation, and people. We must love all that God has chosen to bless, which includes all cultures. Historically, Christian mission, though flawed by destructive failures, has been instrumental in protecting and preserving indigenous cultures and their languages. Godly love, however, also includes critical discernment, for all cultures show not only positive evidence of the image of God in human lives, but also the negative fingerprints of Satan and sin. We long to see the gospel embodied and embedded in all cultures, redeeming them from within so that they may display the glory of God and the radiant fullness of Christ. We look forward to the wealth, glory, and splendour of all cultures being brought into the city of God—redeemed and purged of all sin, enriching the new creation.[26]

Such love for all peoples demands that we reject the evils of racism and ethnocentrism, and treat every ethnic and cultural group with dignity and respect, on the grounds of their value to God in creation and redemption.[27]

Such love also demands that we seek to make the gospel known among every people and culture everywhere. No nation, Jew or Gentile, is exempt from the scope of the great commission. Evangelism is the outflow of hearts that are filled with the love of God for those who do not yet know him. We confess with shame that there are still very many peoples in the world who have never yet heard the message of God's love in Jesus Christ. We renew

---

[26] Acts 17:26; Deuteronomy 32:8; Genesis 10:31–32; 12:3; Revelation 7:9–10; 21:24–27.
[27] Acts 10:35; 14:17; 17:27.

the commitment that has inspired The Lausanne Movement from its beginning, to use every means possible to reach all peoples with the gospel.

C. We love the world's poor and suffering. The Bible tells us that the Lord
is loving toward all he has made, upholds the cause of the oppressed, loves
the foreigner, feeds the hungry, sustains the fatherless and widow.[28] The
Bible also shows that God wills to do these things through human beings
committed to such action. God holds responsible especially those who are
appointed to political or judicial leadership in society,[29] but all God's people
are commanded—by the law and prophets, Psalms and Wisdom, Jesus and
Paul, James and John—to reflect the love and justice of God in practical
love and justice for the needy.[30]

Such love for the poor demands that we not only love mercy and deeds
of compassion, but also that we do justice through exposing and oppos-
ing all that oppresses and exploits the poor. "We must not be afraid to
denounce evil and injustice wherever they exist."[31] We confess with shame
that on this matter we fail to share God's passion, fail to embody God's love,
fail to reflect God's character, and fail to do God's will. We give ourselves
afresh to the promotion of justice, including solidarity and advocacy on behalf of the marginalized and oppressed. We recognize such struggle against
evil as a dimension of spiritual warfare that can only be waged through the
victory of the cross and resurrection, in the power of the Holy Spirit, and
with constant prayer.

D. We love our neighbours as ourselves. Jesus called his disciples to obey
this commandment as the second greatest in the law, but then he radically
deepened the demand (from the same chapter), "love the foreigner as yourself" into "love your enemies."[32]

Such love for our neighbours demands that we respond to all people
out of the heart of the gospel, in obedience to Christ's command and following Christ's example. This love for our neighbours embraces people of other
faiths, and extends to those who hate us, slander and persecute us, and

---

[28] Psalms 145:9, 13, 17; 147:7–9; Deuteronomy 10:17–18.

[29] Genesis 18:19; Exodus 23:6–9; Deuteronomy 16:18–20; Job 29:7–17; Psalms
72:4, 12–14; 82; Proverbs 31:4–9; Jeremiah 22:1–3; Daniel 4:27.

[30] Exodus 22:21–27; Leviticus 19:33–34; Deuteronomy 10:18–19; 15:7–11;
Isaiah 1:16–17; 58:6–9; Amos 5:11–15, 21–24; Psalm 112; Job 31:13–23; Proverbs
14:31; 19:17; 29:7; Matthew 25:31–46; Luke 14:12–14; Galatians 2:10; 2 Corinthians 8–9; Romans 15:25–27; 1 Timothy 6:17–19; James 1:27; 2:14–17; 1 John
3:16–18.

[31] The Lausanne Covenant. Paragraph 5.

[32] Leviticus 19:34; Matthew 5:43–44.

even kill us. Jesus taught us to respond to lies with truth, to those doing evil with acts of kindness, mercy, and forgiveness, to violence and murder against his disciples with self-sacrifice, in order to draw people to him and to break the chain of evil. We emphatically reject the way of violence in the spread of the gospel, and renounce the temptation to retaliate with revenge against those who do us wrong. Such disobedience is incompatible with the example and teaching of Christ and the New Testament.[33] At the same time, our loving duty towards our suffering neighbours requires us to seek justice on their behalf through proper appeal to legal and state authorities who function as God's servants in punishing wrongdoers.[34]

E. *The world we do not love.* The world of God's good creation has become the world of human and satanic rebellion against God. We are commanded not to love that world of sinful desire, greed, and human pride. We confess with sorrow that exactly those marks of worldliness so often disfigure our Christian presence and deny our gospel witness.[35]

*We commit ourselves afresh not to flirt with the fallen world and its transient passions, but to love the whole world as God loves it. So we love the world in holy longing for the redemption and renewal of all creation and all cultures in Christ, the ingathering of God's people from all nations to the ends of the earth, and the ending of all destruction, poverty, and enmity.*

## Overview questions

1. Read Psalm 24:1–2 and Colossians 1:15–20. "The earth is created, sustained, and redeemed by Christ." How then should we treat God's creation? In your culture and in your life, what practices contribute most to the degradation of our world? In your context, what practical steps need to be taken to reverse this damage? What could your local church, or your family, do to improve the environment and social structures and to model care for God's creation? How could the global church work together to challenge some of the vested interests that lead to deforestation, water shortages and growth of desert, pollution, social breakdown, and other ills? Share stories of practical action.

---

[33] Matthew 5:38–39; Luke 6:27–29; 23:34; Romans 12:17–21; 1 Peter 3:18–23; 4:12–16.
[34] Romans 13:4.
[35] 1 John 2:15–17.

## Digging deeper

2. How can Christians be agents of reconciliation between different ethnic groups, tribes, or nations? In your context, who are the groups who are traditionally despised or hated by the majority? How can the Christian community model a different way of relating to those different from ourselves? How in an increasingly mobile world can we develop multicultural church communities?

3. Read Deuteronomy 10:18–19; 15:7–11; and Matthew 25:31–46. What reasons are given for caring especially for the poor and vulnerable? Who are these in your community, and how might Christians express care for them? What practical actions should the global church take to challenge the economic imbalances around the world? If our community is among the poor, what is our responsibility for others in other poor communities?

4. What elements of your culture display rebellion against God? Jesus warned that it is easier to see the splinter in someone else's eye than the plank in our own. Bearing that in mind, what are some of the signs of rebellion against God that you see in other cultures?

5. Invite a person or family from an ethnic group different from your own into your home for a meal. Learn some greetings and basic phrases from them, and ask them to share some folk tales or proverbs or songs from their culture. What do you need to do to build genuine friendship across cultures?

6. Plant a tree, or grow some flowers or vegetables, or organise a neighbourhood "litter-pick" or other community project that improves quality of life for many.

# 8

# WE LOVE THE GOSPEL OF GOD

*As disciples of Jesus, we are gospel people. The core of our identity is our passion for the biblical good news of the saving work of God through Jesus Christ. We are united by our experience of the grace of God in the gospel and by our motivation to make that gospel of grace known to the ends of the earth by every possible means.*

A. *We love the good news in a world of bad news.* The gospel addresses the dire effects of human sin, failure, and need. Human beings rebelled against God, rejected God's authority, and disobeyed God's Word. In this sinful state, we are alienated from God, from one another, and from the created order. Sin deserves God's condemnation. Those who refuse to repent and "do not obey the gospel of our Lord Jesus Christ will be punished with eternal destruction and shut out from the presence of God."[36] The effects of sin and the power of evil have corrupted every dimension of human personhood (spiritual, physical, intellectual, and relational). They have permeated cultural, economic, social, political, and religious life through all cultures and all generations of history. They have caused incalculable misery to the human race and damage to God's creation. Against this bleak background, the biblical gospel is indeed very good news.

B. *We love the story the gospel tells.* The gospel announces as good news the historical events of the life, death, and resurrection of Jesus of Nazareth. As the son of David, the promised Messiah King, Jesus is the one through whom alone God established his kingdom and acted for the salvation of the world, enabling all nations on earth to be blessed, as he promised Abraham. Paul defines the gospel in stating that "Christ died for our sins according to the scriptures, that he was buried, that he was raised on the third day, according the scriptures, and that he appeared to Peter and

---

[36] Genesis 3; 2 Thessalonians 1:9.

then to the Twelve." The gospel declares that, on the cross of Christ, God took upon himself, in the person of his Son and in our place, the judgment our sin deserves. In the same great saving act, completed, vindicated, and declared through the resurrection, God won the decisive victory over Satan, death, and all evil powers, liberated us from their power and fear, and ensured their eventual destruction. God accomplished the reconciliation of believers with himself and with one another across all boundaries and enmities. God also accomplished his purpose of the ultimate reconciliation of all creation, and in the bodily resurrection of Jesus has given us the first fruits of the new creation. "God was in Christ reconciling the world to himself." [37] How we love the gospel story!

*C. We love the assurance the gospel brings.* Solely through trusting in Christ alone, we are united with Christ through the Holy Spirit and are counted righteous in Christ before God. Being justified by faith we have peace with God and no longer face condemnation. We receive the forgiveness of our sins. We are born again into a living hope by sharing Christ's risen life. We are adopted as fellow heirs with Christ. We become citizens of God's covenant people, members of God's family, and the place of God's dwelling. So by trusting in Christ, we have full assurance of salvation and eternal life, for our salvation ultimately depends, not on ourselves, but on the work of Christ and the promise of God. "Nothing in all creation will be able to separate us from the love of God that is in Christ Jesus our Lord."[38] How we love the gospel's promise!

*D. We love the transformation the gospel produces.* The gospel is God's life-transforming power at work in the world. "It is the power of God for the salvation of everyone who believes."[39] Faith alone is the means by which the blessings and assurance of the gospel are received. Saving faith however never remains alone, but necessarily shows itself in obedience. Christian obedience is "faith expressing itself through love."[40] We are not saved by good works, but having been saved by grace alone we are "created in Christ Jesus to do good works."[41] "Faith by itself, if it is not accompanied by action, is dead."[42] Paul saw the ethical transformation that the gospel produces as

---

[37] Mark 1:1, 14–15; Romans 1:1–4; 4; 1 Corinthians 15:3–5; 1 Peter 2:24; Colossians 2:15; Hebrews 2:14–15; Ephesians 2:14–18; Colossians 1:20; 2 Corinthians 5:19.
[38] Romans 4; Philippians 3:1–11; Romans 5:1–2; 8:1–4; Ephesians 1:7; Colossians 1:13–14; 1 Peter 1:3; Galatians 3:26–4:7; Ephesians 2:19–22; John 20:30–31; 1 John 5:12–13; Romans 8:31–39.
[39] Romans 1:16.
[40] Galatians 5:6.
[41] Ephesians 2:10.
[42] James 2:17.

the work of God's grace—grace which achieved our salvation at Christ's first coming, and grace that teaches us to live ethically in the light of his second coming.[43] For Paul, "obeying the gospel" meant both trusting in grace, and then being taught by grace.[44] Paul's missional goal was to bring about "the obedience of faith" among all nations.[45] This strongly covenantal language recalls Abraham. Abraham believed God's promise, which was credited to him as righteousness, and then obeyed God's command in demonstration of his faith. "By faith Abraham . . . obeyed."[46] Repentance and faith in Jesus Christ are the first acts of obedience the gospel calls for; ongoing obedience to God's commands is the way of life that gospel faith enables, through the sanctifying Holy Spirit.[47] Obedience is thus the living proof of saving faith and the living fruit of it. Obedience is also the test of our love for Jesus. "Whoever has my commands and obeys them, he is the one who loves me."[48] "We know that we have come to know him if we obey his commands."[49] How we love the gospel's power!

## Overview questions

1. What makes "sin" sin? Read John 1:29; 8:34; Romans 1:18–25; 1 John 1:8–2:2; and 2 Thessalonians 1:7–10. How is sin qualitatively different from "just being a bit naughty"? What are its consequences in this present life and eternally? How does this make the gospel the best news ever? At the heart of the gospel is the Person of our Lord Jesus Christ. How would you tell his story to a friend who has never heard it? We need the whole story to have a complete picture, but how would you summarise the key events? As you pray for your friends, what means might the Lord use to reveal himself to them?

---

[43] Titus 2:11–14.
[44] Romans 15:18–19; 16:19; 2 Corinthians 9:13.
[45] Romans 1:5; 16:26.
[46] Genesis 15:6; Galatians 6:6–9; Hebrews 11:8; Genesis 22:15–18; James 2:20–24.
[47] Romans 8:4.
[48] John 14:21.
[49] 1 John 2:3.

## Digging deeper

2. What do we need to do to enter into the life of the gospel? How will we know that we have eternal life? What will be the evidences of genuine faith?

3. Because the gospel is good news, and so crucial both for the glory of God and the well-being of people and creation, how can our Christian communities become profoundly missional (i.e., eagerly proclaiming and living out the gospel)? What do you and your church need to be and do? If you are not steadily reaching people for Christ, what needs to change?

4. The gospel, properly understood and responded to, leads to wholistic personal transformation, and Christians together should be agents of transformation for the community. What do you and your local church do to seek greater justice and human flourishing for the wider community? How do we do it "in the name of Jesus," so that proclamation and action come together?

5. Read 2 Corinthians 9:12–15. How do obedience, love, and sharing the gospel relate to one another? Give some examples from everyday life.

# 9

# WE LOVE THE PEOPLE OF GOD

*The people of God are those from all ages and all nations whom God in Christ has loved, chosen, called, saved, and sanctified as a people for his own possession, to share in the glory of Christ as citizens of the new creation. As those, then, whom God has loved from eternity to eternity and throughout all our turbulent and rebellious history, we are commanded to love one another. For "since God so loved us, we also ought to love one another," and thereby "be imitators of God . . . and live a life of love, just as Christ loved us and gave himself up for us" Love for one another in the family of God is not merely a desirable option but an inescapable command. Such love is the first evidence of obedience to the gospel, the necessary expression of our submission to Christ's Lordship, and a potent engine of world mission.*[50]

A. *Love calls for unity.* Jesus' command that his disciples should love one another is linked to his prayer that they should be one. Both the command and the prayer are missional—"that the world may know you are my disciples," and that "the world may know that you [the Father] sent me."[51] A most powerfully convincing mark of the truth of the gospel is when Christian believers are united in love across the barriers of the world's inveterate divisions—barriers of race, colour, gender, social class, economic privilege, or political alignment. However, few things so destroy our testimony as when Christians mirror and amplify the very same divisions among themselves. We urgently seek a new global partnership within the body of Christ across all continents, rooted in profound mutual love, mutual submission, and dramatic economic sharing without paternalism or unhealthy dependency. And we seek this not only as a demonstration of our unity in the

---

[50] 2 Thessalonians 2:13–14; 1 John 4:11; Ephesians 5:2; 1 Thessalonians 1:3; 4:9–10; John 13:35.
[51] John 13:34–35; 17:21.

gospel, but also for the sake of the name of Christ and the mission of God in all the world.

B. *Love calls for honesty.* Love speaks truth with grace. No one loved God's people more than the prophets of Israel and Jesus himself. Yet no one confronted them more honestly with the truth of their failure, idolatry, and rebellion against their covenant Lord. And in doing so, they called God's people to repent, so that they could be forgiven and restored to the service of God's mission. The same voice of prophetic love must be heard today, for the same reason. Our love for the Church of God aches with grief over the ugliness among us that so disfigures the face of our dear Lord Jesus Christ and hides his beauty from the world—the world that so desperately needs to be drawn to him.

C. *Love calls for solidarity.* Loving one another includes especially caring for those who are persecuted and in prison for their faith and witness. If one part of the body suffers, all parts suffer with it. We are all, like John, "companions in the suffering and kingdom and patient endurance that are ours in Jesus."[52] We commit ourselves to share in the suffering of members of the body of Christ throughout the world, through information, prayer, advocacy, and other means of support. We see such sharing, however, not merely as an exercise of pity, but longing also to learn what the suffering Church can teach and give to those parts of Christ's body that are not suffering in the same way. We are warned that the Church that feels itself at ease in its wealth and self-sufficiency may, like Laodicea, be the Church that Jesus sees as the most blind to its own poverty, and from which he himself feels a stranger outside the door.[53]

*Jesus calls all his disciples together to be one family among the nations, a reconciled fellowship in which all sinful barriers are broken down through his reconciling grace. This Church is a community of grace, obedience, and love in the communion of the Holy Spirit, in which the glorious attributes of God and gracious characteristics of Christ are reflected and God's multi-coloured wisdom is displayed. As the most vivid present expression of the kingdom of God, the Church is the community of the reconciled who no longer live for themselves, but for the Saviour who loved them and gave himself for them.*

---

[52] Hebrews 13:1–3; 1 Corinthians 12:26; Revelation 1:9.
[53] Revelation 3:17–20.

## Overview questions

1. Read John 13:34–35 and John 17:21. Why is Jesus so passionate that his disciples should love one another? The disunity of God's people is one of the commonest reasons given by unbelievers in some parts of the world for not listening to the gospel: "Why should we believe you when you can't even agree among yourselves?" In what practical ways can we build better relationships in our contexts between different congregations and denominations?

## Digging deeper

2. In your context, what are the issues which lead to the most disunity and lack of harmony between Christians? Which issues are doctrinal? How do you seek to resolve them? Which issues are cultural or matters of temperament? How do you seek to resolve them? Many divisions came from particular historical situations. How, when, and to what extent can we move on from these? Give some practical examples.

3. The CTC speaks of the need for "prophetic love." What does this mean? What do you think are the issues that Jesus would call us to repent of, in your context and for the global church? How could we speak out prophetically, but with grace and humility, in our situations?

4. How can we express meaningful solidarity with Christian brothers and sisters who suffer because of persecution and because they along with their whole population are suffering (e.g., at a time of famine or natural disaster)?

5. In a world where globalisation is often a problem, the global church should be the one true expression of a healthy global community. How can the church develop relationships from which exploitation and abuse of power or wealth (or poverty) have been banished? What steps do we need to take to bring this about?

# 10

# WE LOVE THE MISSION OF GOD

*We are committed to world mission, because it is central to our understanding of God, the Bible, the Church, human history, and the ultimate future. The whole Bible reveals the mission of God to bring all things in heaven and earth into unity under Christ, reconciling them through the blood of his cross. In fulfilling his mission, God will transform the creation broken by sin and evil into the new creation in which there is no more sin or curse. God will fulfil his promise to Abraham to bless all nations on the earth, through the gospel of Jesus, the Messiah, the seed of Abraham. God will transform the fractured world of nations that are scattered under the judgment of God into the new humanity that will be redeemed by the blood of Christ from every tribe, nation, people, and language, and will be gathered to worship our God and Saviour. God will destroy the reign of death, corruption, and violence when Christ returns to establish his eternal reign of life, justice, and peace. Then God, Immanuel, will dwell with us, and the kingdom of the world will become the kingdom of our Lord and of his Christ and he shall reign for ever and ever.*[54]

A. *Our participation in God's mission.* God calls his people to share his mission. The Church from all nations stands in continuity through the Messiah Jesus with God's people in the Old Testament. With them we have been called through Abraham and commissioned to be a blessing and a light to the nations. With them, we are to be shaped and taught through the law and the prophets to be a community of holiness, compassion, and justice in a world of sin and suffering. We have been redeemed through the cross and resurrection of Jesus Christ, and empowered by the Holy Spirit to bear witness to what God has done in Christ. The Church exists to worship and glorify God for all eternity and to participate in the transforming mission of God within history. Our mission is wholly derived from God's mission, addresses the whole of God's creation, and is grounded at its centre in

---

[54] Ephesians 1:9–10; Colossians 1:20; Genesis 1–12; Revelation 21–22.

the redeeming victory of the cross. This is the people to whom we belong, whose faith we confess and whose mission we share.

B. *The integrity of our mission.* The source of all our mission is what God has done in Christ for the redemption of the whole world, as revealed in the Bible. Our evangelistic task is to make that good news known to all nations. The context of all our mission is the world in which we live, the world of sin, suffering, injustice, and creational disorder, into which God sends us to love and serve for Christ's sake. All our mission must therefore reflect the integration of evangelism and committed engagement in the world, both being ordered and driven by the whole biblical revelation of the gospel of God.

> Evangelism itself is the proclamation of the historical, biblical Christ as Saviour and Lord, with a view to persuading people to come to him personally and so be reconciled to God. . . . The results of evangelism include obedience to Christ, incorporation into his Church and responsible service in the world. . . . We affirm that evangelism and socio-political involvement are both part of our Christian duty. For both are necessary expressions of our doctrines of God and humankind, our love for our neighbour and our obedience to Jesus Christ. . . . The salvation we proclaim should be transforming us in the totality of our personal and social responsibilities. Faith without works is dead.[55]

> Integral mission is the proclamation and demonstration of the gospel. It is not simply that evangelism and social involvement are to be done alongside each other. Rather, in integral mission our proclamation has social consequences as we call people to love and repentance in all areas of life. And our social involvement has evangelistic consequences as we bear witness to the transforming grace of Jesus Christ. If we ignore the world, we betray the Word of God which sends us out to serve the world. If we ignore the Word of God, we have nothing to bring to the world.[56]

*We commit ourselves to the integral and dynamic exercise of all dimensions of mission to which God calls his Church.*

> ▷ *God commands us to make known to all nations the truth of God's revelation and the gospel of God's saving grace through Jesus Christ, calling all people to repentance, faith, baptism, and obedient discipleship.*

> ▷ *God commands us to reflect his own character through compassionate care for the needy, and to demonstrate the values and the power of the kingdom of God in striving for justice and peace and in caring for God's creation.*

---

[55] *The Lausanne Covenant,* Paragraphs 4 and 5.
[56] *The Micah Declaration on Integral Mission.*

*In response to God's boundless love for us in Christ, and out of our overflowing love for him, we rededicate ourselves, with the help of the Holy Spirit, fully to obey all that God commands, with self-denying humility, joy and courage. We renew this covenant with the Lord—the Lord we love because he first loved us.*

## Overview questions

1. When you hear the word "mission," what do you think of? Read Ephesians 1:9–10 and Colossians 1:15–20. What do these passages teach us about the big picture of mission? The church is called to share in God's mission, not to invent its own. In what ways do we invent our own? What must we do to be sure that we are sharing in God's mission? How should we establish priorities?

## Digging deeper

2. In the book of Revelation, the Holy Spirit inspires the Apostle John to paint a picture of what "the new heavens and the new earth" will look like when history as we know it comes to an end and the will of God is perfectly fulfilled. How does the ministry of Jesus in the Gospels illustrate what that perfect will of God looks like in our present fallen world? What practical things can we do to reflect that perfect will of God in our contexts?

3. Being missionary people is not optional; it's part of being made in the image of God who is a missionary God. How can you encourage your local church to be fully engaged in mission locally and globally? Tell stories to encourage one another. Pray for greater discernment to recognise the people God is stirring up to seek him, and for courage and zeal to follow the Holy Spirit's leading.

4. There are still people groups which have no known gospel witness, and many more where injustice, oppression, poverty, or other suffering prevails. Together with your local church community, what could you do to change at least one of these situations? Agree some specific action—and decide on the next steps.

# Part II

# FOR THE WORLD WE SERVE: THE CAPE TOWN CALL TO ACTION

# INTRODUCTION

Our covenant with God binds love and obedience together. God rejoices to see our "work produced by faith" and our "labour prompted by love,"[57] for "we are God's workmanship, created in Christ Jesus to do good works, which God prepared in advance for us to do."[58]

As members of the worldwide Church of Jesus Christ, we have sought to listen to the voice of God through the Holy Spirit. We have listened to his voice coming to us from his written Word in the exposition of Ephesians, and through the voices of his people around the world. Our six major Congress themes provide a framework to discern the challenges facing the worldwide Church of Christ, and our priorities for the future. We do not imply that these commitments are the only ones the Church should consider, or that priorities everywhere are the same.

---

[57] 1 Thessalonians 1:3.
[58] Ephesians 2:10.

# IIA

# Bearing Witness to the Truth of Christ in a Pluralistic, Globalized World

## 1. Truth and the Person of Christ

Jesus Christ is the truth of the universe. Because Jesus is truth, truth in Christ is (1) personal as well as propositional; (2) universal as well as contextual; (3) ultimate as well as present.

### Christian truth

*Personal and propositional.* There is no false dichotomy between these, and neither should be emphasized at the expense of the other. To affirm "Truth is the Person of Christ" is itself a proposition that we claim to be true, as are all the great affirmations of our faith: "God is love"; "Jesus is Lord." But these truths can be fully known only in personal relationship with God through Christ, in worship, love, and obedience.

*Universal and local.* The truth of Christ is universal because he is Creator and Lord of all. But it is also local, for Christ is being formed in the hearts and lives of believers of all cultures, enabling them to shine the light of his transforming truth into all contexts.

*Ultimate and present.* Christ is the ultimate truth, for the cosmic plan of God is to integrate all created reality under the Lordship of Christ. But Christ is the source of all truth in the present because the universe is created and sustained by him, and he reigns as risen and ascended Lord over all powers and authorities.[59]

---

[59] Ephesians 1:10, 20–21.

Some cultures reject the whole idea of a singular truth. This can happen under the influence of the ideology of relativistic pluralism, or as an understandable reaction to the evil of totalitarian systems that proclaim a "singular truth," with arrogance and violent oppression against all who resist it.

The only singular truth to which we bear witness is not an oppressive system, but the person of Jesus of Nazareth. He lived as the truth, but used no force of arms or angels. He came to a stable and went to a cross. People accepted or rejected him, understood or misinterpreted him, followed him or walked away. He had no stronger weapons than his own presence in words and good works. Jesus spoke truth into the lives of sinners, Gentiles, women, the sick, the marginalized and rejected, as well as the self-righteous, the rich, and the powerful. But in so doing he brought a greater truth, the gift of God's saving truth—himself, received by faith. When Jesus spoke truth he granted truth. The ultimate truth of Jesus was exposed when he suffered on the cross for God's truth to prevail over the devil's lies. In his resurrection God vindicated the truth of Christ for all people and all creation for all time.

We are shamed by those within the Christian community who downplay the importance of truth, who scornfully deny or casually dismiss what our Lord declared, what the Scriptures defend, and what our sisters and brothers die for rather than deny.

## A. As disciples of Christ we are called to be people of truth.

1. We must *live* the truth. To live the truth is to be the face of Jesus, through whom the glory of the gospel is revealed to blinded minds. People will see truth in the faces of those who live their lives for Jesus, in faithfulness and love.

2. We must *proclaim* the truth. Spoken proclamation of the truth of the gospel remains paramount in our mission. This cannot be separated from living out the truth. Works and words must go together.

## B. We urge church leaders, pastors, and evangelists to preach and teach the fullness of the biblical gospel as Paul did, in all its cosmic scope and truth. We must present the gospel not merely as offering individual salvation, or a better solution to needs than other gods can provide, but as God's plan for the whole universe in Christ. People sometimes come to Christ to meet a personal need, but they stay with Christ when they find him to be the truth.

## Overview questions

1. Why is truth so important? What are the main factors in your culture and context which oppose the concept of "absolute truth," and especially biblical truth? In the face of them, how would you robustly explain that Jesus *is* truth? In some cultures, the question is not whether or not Jesus is God and truth but whose side is he on. How does biblical revelation help to answer that?

## Digging deeper

2. How can we try to ensure that the truth we pass along to others, in word and deed, is not distorted by our cultural assumptions? What must we do to try to ensure that our understanding and interpretation of Scripture are what the Holy Spirit meant as he inspired the writers? What should we do when our understanding differs from someone else's?

3. What practical steps do you take to study the whole of Scripture, not just your favourite passages? Why does it matter? If you are a congregational leader or preacher, how do you organise your teaching so as to cover "the whole counsel of God"?

4. How does the death and resurrection of our Lord Jesus help us to be sure that he is the truth? Read Acts 2:14–41. How does Peter explain Jesus' identity to a Jewish audience? Read Acts 17:16–36. How does Paul explain Jesus' identity to one specific Gentile audience? Which parts of these sermons are most helpful in your culture in explaining Jesus' identity?

5. "People sometimes *come* to Christ to meet a personal need, but they *stay* with Christ when they find him to be the truth." Does this observation fit in your cultural situation? How do you think we can help one another to "find him to be the truth," both in study and worship and in proven experience?

## 2. Truth and the challenge of pluralism

Cultural and religious plurality is a fact, and Christians in Asia, for example, have lived with it for centuries. Different religions each affirm that theirs is the way of truth. Most will seek to respect competing truth claims of other faiths and live alongside them. However, postmodern, relativist pluralism is different. Its ideology allows for no absolute or universal truth. While tolerating truth claims, it views them as no more than cultural constructs. (This position is logically self-destroying for it affirms as a single absolute truth that there is no single absolute truth.) Such pluralism asserts "tolerance" as an ultimate value, but it can take oppressive forms in countries where secularism or aggressive atheism governs the public arena.

### Lessons from history

We urge Christians in all parts of the world to learn the lessons of history. In places where Christianity is presently strong, we should not ignore the seed of ideological secularism, even when it seems to affect only a small proportion of the population. The church in some parts of the West has declined, partly because the church's response to Enlightenment modernity was either to compromise with it and surrender the distinctive claims of transcendent biblical truth or to withdraw from the public arena into a marginal realm of private piety and religious activity.

### The Apostle Peter's example

We must follow the example of Peter, whose proclamation of the truth in Acts 2 was public, biblical, reasonable, historical, and convincing.

A. We long to see greater commitment to the hard work of robust apologetics. This must be at two levels.

1. We need to identify, equip, and pray for those who can engage at the highest intellectual and public level in arguing for and defending biblical truth in the public arena.

2. We urge Church leaders and pastors to equip all believers with the courage and the tools to relate the truth with prophetic relevance to everyday public conversation, and so to engage every aspect of the culture we live in.

## Overview questions

1. If you live in a culture strongly dominated by a religion other than Christianity, how do you respond to competing truth claims? What are some of the most effective ways to bear witness to Jesus Christ and his uniqueness as the only path for reconciliation with God in such a context? What are some of the difficulties?

## Digging deeper

2. If you live in a multicultural society, where people of many different faiths live alongside one another, how should Christians respond to the challenges and the opportunities? How can we show genuine love and care to those of other faiths while still standing firm on the uniqueness of Jesus Christ as only Saviour?

3. If you live in a society now dominated by postmodern relativism, what are the challenges and the opportunities for faithful, creative witness? How does postmodernity undermine biblical truth and morality? What consequences should we expect?

4. How can we develop apologists—those who can defend biblical truth—for the public arena: politicians who form far-reaching policies, university and school teachers who shape people's minds, media people who also shape people's minds? Pause and pray for any Christians you know about in these and similarly influential roles.

5. Christian truth relates to the whole of life. In our personal Bible study and in preaching and teaching in the church, how can we make sure that we not only nourish personal faith and worship but also equip one another to live lives transformed in every part of life by God's truth?

# 3. Truth and the workplace

The Bible shows us God's truth about human work as part of God's good purpose in creation. The Bible brings the whole of our working lives within the sphere of ministry, as we serve God in different callings. By contrast, the falsehood of a "sacred-secular divide" has permeated the Church's thinking and action. This divide tells us that religious activity belongs to God, whereas other activity does not. Most Christians spend most of their time in work which they may think has little spiritual value (so-called secular work). But God is Lord of all of life. "Whatever you do, work at it with all your heart, as working for the Lord, not for men,"[60] said Paul, to slaves in the pagan workplace.

## *A biblical perspective of work*

The creation narrative shows us God the worker. Human beings, made in the image of God, are co-workers with God. We are mandated to rule over God's creation, to use its abundance responsibly for our needs, to serve and care for the earth. Work takes many forms: the work of the home; subsistence farming; serving the family, village, or community; paid employment;

---

[60] Colossians 3:23.

and even the efforts of those without employment. God's calling can include honest work in any place or form and such work is ministry—serving God and society. The Bible focuses extensively on the world of work. God audits the arenas of public and private work and will ultimately redeem the fruit of human work, purged of all sin and evil, for the glory of the new creation.[61] It is unbiblical to create a division of "clergy" and "laity," as if the ministry and mission of the church is the work of church-paid professionals—"ministers" and "missionaries."

The church often lacks commitment to whole-life disciple making. Jesus did not come to redeem our leisure time, but all of our time. And work done with such an ethical and redemptive understanding "will make the teaching about God our Saviour attractive."[62]

In spite of the enormous evangelistic and transformational opportunity of the workplace, where adult Christians have most relationships with non-Christians, few churches have the vision to equip their people to seize this. We have failed to regard work in itself as biblically and intrinsically significant, as we have failed to bring the whole of life under the Lordship of Christ.

A. *We name this secular-sacred divide as a major obstacle to the mobilization of all God's people in the mission of God,* and we call upon Christians worldwide to reject its unbiblical assumptions and resist its damaging effects. We challenge the tendency to see ministry and mission (local and cross-cultural) as being mainly the work of church-paid ministers and missionaries, who are a tiny percentage of the whole body of Christ.

B. *We encourage all believers to accept and affirm their own daily ministry and mission as being wherever God has called them to work.* We challenge pastors and church leaders to support people in such ministry—in the community and in the workplace—"to equip the saints for works of service [ministry]"—in every part of their lives.

C. *We need intensive efforts to train all God's people in whole-life discipleship,* which means to live, think, work, and speak from a biblical worldview and with missional effectiveness in every place or circumstance of daily life and work.

---

[61] Revelation 21:24–26.
[62] Titus 2:10.

Christians in many skills, trades, businesses, and professions can often go to places where traditional church planters and evangelists may not. What these "tentmakers" and business people do in the workplace must be valued as an aspect of the ministry of local churches.

*D. We urge church leaders to understand the strategic impact of ministry in the workplace* and to mobilize, equip, and send out their church members as missionaries into the workplace, both in their own local communities and in countries that are closed to traditional forms of gospel witness.

*E. We urge mission leaders to integrate "tentmakers" fully into the global missional strategy.*

## Overview questions

1. Read Genesis 1:27–30 and Genesis 2:15. What do you think God meant when he said people were to "subdue" the earth (Genesis 1:28), and to "work it and take care of it" (Genesis 2:15)? This side of the Fall, how do you think we can obey this? How has the world abused these commands? Read Colossians 3:23–24. Why was this command so remarkable for its original hearers? How can you fulfil your daily occupation, whatever it may be, and whether it is pleasant or not, so that you are serving the Lord and bearing witness to the gospel?

## Digging deeper

2. Work is clearly a good thing in God's eyes, and in many cultures unemployment causes significant problems. What could your Christian community do to create satisfying employment, both paid and unpaid?

3. Why is the "sacred-secular" divide a falsehood? How can you break down this false idea in your life, and how can you encourage others to do so also? What might be the effect on the church's effectiveness if we really grasped this?

4. What practical steps could pastors take to "equip the saints for works of service" in their various workplaces? Why do you think this so rarely happens? What needs to change?

5. Missionary service is frequently assumed to be either evangelism or church planting. Why is this an inadequate understanding of cross-cultural mission? Should tentmakers and business people go only to places where evangelists and church planters cannot go? How could they complement one another for more effective mission, in "open access" contexts as well? If you are a mission agency leader, how should this shape your recruitment? If you are a church leader, how should this affect your understanding of who is a missionary and who isn't?

## 4. Truth and the globalized media

We commit ourselves to a renewed critical and creative engagement with media and technology, as part of making the case for the truth of Christ in our media cultures. We must do so as God's ambassadors of truth, grace, love, peace, and justice.

We identify the following major needs:

A. *Media awareness:* to help people develop a more critical awareness of the messages they receive, and of the worldview behind them. The media can be neutral, and sometimes gospel-friendly. But they are also used for pornography, violence, and greed. We encourage pastors and churches to face these issues openly and to provide teaching and guidance for believers in resisting such pressures and temptations.

B. *Media presence:* to develop authentic and credible Christian role models and communicators for the general news media and the entertainment media, and to commend these careers as a worthy means of influence for Christ.

C. *Media ministries:* to develop creative, combined and interactive use of "traditional," "old," and "new" media, to communicate the gospel of Christ in the context of a holistic biblical worldview.

## Digital communication

We acknowledge that in many parts of the world the primary means of communication is still either face to face through the spoken word or through the printed word. However, the digital revolution is bringing instant mass communication of enormous complexity, speed, and multiplicity of content. The Global South is being rapidly impacted by globalization with digital information technology as its key carrier. Wherever technology goes, the news and entertainment media follow, with underlying secular and religious worldviews. The church around the world is increasingly facing a missional encounter with globalization in general and technology and media specifically. To be prepared for such an encounter there is an urgent need to understand and apply the Christian worldview in response to all types of media. The communication of the gospel is and always has been mediated in various ways. The resources and tools through which that mediation takes place require careful Christian analysis and discernment, since the medium of communication can easily distort the message.

## Overview questions

1. What are the chief ways of communicating in your culture? How is modern technology changing traditional patterns of communication? Do the younger generation(s) communicate differently from the older generation(s); the rich differently from the poor? How is this affecting the church in your context? What are the potential gains? Are there things to guard against?

## Digging deeper

2. What are the worldviews and values conveyed by the dominant media in your context? Are they gospel-friendly, neutral, or undermining biblical truth? How can we critique them more carefully? What practical steps could you take in your context to influence media for good?

3. Which modern media and technological changes can we gladly adopt for effective evangelism and teaching? How do you, your church, or your mission agency use them? How do you evaluate their effectiveness? What might be some pitfalls?

4. Some modern technology is very expensive. How can we develop good partnerships between different agencies and churches to share resources of money, skill, and personnel? How could that work in your context?

5. What practical steps could you and your Christian community take to support Christians who work in influential media—books, films, television, radio, or newspapers? What can you do to encourage a new generation of Christians in media roles? How would you help them to integrate biblical truth and values in their work, especially where they work for employers who do not share those values?

# 5. Truth and the arts in mission

We possess the gift of creativity because we bear the image of God. Art in its many forms is an integral part of what we do as humans and can reflect something of the beauty and truth of God. Artists at their best are truth-tellers and so the arts constitute one important way in which we can speak the truth of the gospel. Drama, dance, story, music, and visual image can be expressions both of the reality of our brokenness, and of the hope that is centred in the gospel that all things will be made new.

## Mission and the arts

The creation mandate directs us to be culture makers. The Scriptures speak to us through the literary art forms of narrative, poetry, image, and metaphor. And the Church has always engaged image and symbol as well as the word to open to us the truths of the biblical story. Jesus spoke of his own mission in metaphor and parable with the invitation to hear and see the meaning of his presence in the world.

In the context of mission, art is able to bridge our differences and cross cultural barriers. It provides a way to explore the deep and important human questions, which are ultimately religious questions. The divine gift of creativity and imagination has often been a key resource in fostering reconciliation and healing for our human brokenness. This is so in part because creativity and imagination call us to see things in a new way. The invitation of the gospel has that same character. The gospel calls us to enter into a relationship where old things have passed away and all things have become new. This is a path that requires human imagination; that ability to see what is possible through the renewing power of the gospel. The arts then may serve as symbols of hope in an uncertain world. In this respect they resonate with the work of the Holy Spirit. In the great mission of God the Spirit now directs us toward a hopeful future.

In the world of mission, the arts are an untapped resource. We actively encourage greater Christian involvement in the arts.

*A. We long to see the Church in all cultures energetically engaging the arts as a context for mission by:*

1. Bringing the arts back into the life of the faith community as a valid and valuable component of our call to discipleship;

2. Supporting those with artistic gifts, especially sisters and brothers in Christ, so that they may flourish in their work;

3. Letting the arts serve as an hospitable environment in which we can acknowledge and come to know the neighbour and the stranger;

4. Respecting cultural differences and celebrating indigenous artistic expression.

## Overview questions

1. Read 1 Chronicles 15:16, 2 Chronicles 2:7, 2 Chronicles 34:10–13, and Psalm 33:1–3. What do these passages tell us about God's delight in beauty in music, in skilled woodwork and other crafts? How can you incorporate full use of all the arts and celebrate God's gifts in giving creativity, in your evangelism and in the life of your Christian community?

## Digging deeper

2. How can we make our homes and places of worship beautiful, in simple ways and without spending much money? Why is it important to the human spirit to be surrounded by beauty rather than by ugliness? How could beauty be nurtured even in places of great ugliness or extreme poverty such as refugee camps or shanty towns?

3. In your culture, which are the art forms most valued: poetry, music, drama, storytelling, dance, or another? The Bible shows examples of them all, and more. How could you use these better in sharing the gospel with those who do not yet believe and in discipling believers?

4. In your Christian community, arrange an arts celebration and invite the neighbourhood to see and hear what you create: paintings, weaving, stories, songs, or carvings. How could you use this arts celebration as a bridge for the gospel?

5. The Psalms were originally composed to be sung as well as said. The Lord's people have always expressed themselves, their worship, their faith, and their longings through singing. How can poetry set to music reinforce our faith, communally and individually? Are all forms of music, and every instrument, used in your culture suitable for adapting for Christian use? Give your reasons.

## 6. Truth, science, and emerging technologies

This century is widely known as "the Bio-tech Century," with advances in all the emerging technologies (bio, info/digital, nano, virtual reality, artificial intelligence, and robotics). This has deep implications for the Church and for mission, particularly in relation to the biblical truth of what it means to be human. We need to promote authentically Christian responses and practical action in the arena of public policies, to ensure that science and technology are used not to manipulate, distort, and destroy, but to preserve and better fulfil our humanness, as those whom God has created in his own image. We call on:

A. *Local church leaders* to (1) encourage, support, and ask questions of church members who are professionally engaged in science, technology, healthcare, and public policy, and (2) to present to theologically thoughtful students the need for Christians to enter these arenas.

B. *Seminaries* to engage with these fields in their curricula, so future Church leaders and theological educators develop an informed Christian critique of the new technologies.

*C. Theologians, and Christians in government, business, academia, and technical fields,* to form national or regional "think tanks" or partnerships to engage with new technologies and scientific advances, and to speak into the shaping of public policy with a voice that is biblical and relevant.

*D. All local Christian communities* to demonstrate respect for the unique dignity and sanctity of human life, by practical and holistic caring which integrates the physical, emotional, relational, and spiritual aspects of our created humanity.

## Overview questions

1.  In what specific ways are emerging technologies and developments in science affecting your country and culture? Which are the issues that most deeply challenge biblical truth? In what ways? Where do you think these developments may lead? Which are the emerging technologies and scientific advances which may be most helpful for human flourishing in your culture? How can the church support and use these for kingdom purposes? How can the church actively engage with developments and help shape them in ways that glorify God?

## Digging deeper

2.  Read Genesis 1:27–31. What do you think it means that we are made "in the image of God"? What is distinctive about human beings in the whole of creation? How are we like animals; and how are we different? How should this affect our thinking about bio-technology in particular? Are there boundaries that we should seek to set? In your culture, how would you try to influence public policy in these areas?

3. Healthcare is radically different in different parts of the world, its quality and effectiveness usually relating to poverty or wealth, but sometimes to religious views or values associated with gender. What is the underlying worldview in your culture shaping healthcare and how it is done? What are the strengths and weaknesses of modern western "scientific" medicine? What are the strengths and weaknesses of traditional medicine as practised in some parts of the world? What could they learn from one another? What practical steps could most improve healthcare in the poorest parts of the world? What could the world church do together to improve the situation?

4. How is information technology changing our world? In what ways is this influence good, and in what ways is it harmful? In what ways can information technology be used in world mission today? Are there ways in which it undermines Christian truth and values? Are there specific things we need to avoid?

## 7. Truth and the public arenas

The interlocking arenas of government, business, and academia have a strong influence on the values of each nation and, in human terms, define the freedom of the Church.

A. *We encourage Christ-followers to be actively engaged in these spheres,* both in public service or private enterprise, in order to shape societal values and influence public debate. We encourage support for Christ-centred schools and universities that are committed to academic excellence and biblical truth.

B. *Corruption is condemned in the Bible.* It undermines economic development, distorts fair decision-making, and destroys social cohesion. No nation is free of corruption. We invite Christians in the workplace, especially young entrepreneurs, to think creatively about how they can best stand against this scourge.

*C. We encourage young Christian academics to consider a long-term career in the secular university,* to (1) teach and (2) develop their discipline from a biblical worldview, thereby to influence their subject field. We dare not neglect the Academy.[63]

## Overview questions

1. God's intention is for human governments to punish evil and encourage good, but many governments today do not do that. Whether your government is just or unjust, how do you seek to witness to God's truth and influence it and your society for good? If your government persecutes or ill-treats believers or those who protest in some way, how do you pray and act to bring about change? If your government treats its citizens reasonably fairly, and you have freedom of speech, how do you pray and act to bring about change where it is needed and advocate for those who suffer in other countries?

## Digging deeper

2. In what ways does corruption show itself in your culture? What pressures do you experience to join in the corruption? How do you stand against that? In what ways is that difficult or costly in your society? How can you actively model working and living justly? How can Christians in your culture work together to expose corrupt practices and to press for change? Be honest and practical about cheating, lying, stealing, bribery, and other forms of corruption. Pray for one another.

---

[63] "The university is a clear-cut fulcrum with which to move the world. The Church can render no greater service to itself and to the cause of the gospel than to try to recapture the universities for Christ. More potently than by any other means, change the university and you change the world." Charles Habib Malik, former president of the UN General Assembly, in his *1981 Pascal Lectures, A Christian Critique of the University.*

3. Watch the film *Amazing Grace* about William Wilberforce's long campaign against Britain's involvement in the slave trade in the early nineteenth century, or find an inspiring story of someone in your country who brought about great change for good as a result of Christian conviction. How did this person set about the task? What can you learn that could encourage you to pray and work for change, even at high levels of government policy, in your current culture?

4. Why is it so strategic to have Christians working at high levels in the academic and professional worlds? How could your fellowship encourage them and pray for them? If it is not already happening in your country, how could they be helped to network together for greater influence?

# IIB

## BUILDING THE PEACE OF CHRIST IN OUR DIVIDED AND BROKEN WORLD

### 1. The peace that Christ made

Reconciliation to God is inseparable from reconciliation to one another. Christ, who *is* our peace, *made* peace through the cross, and *preached* peace to the divided world of Jew and Gentile. The unity of the people of God is both a fact ("he made the two one"), and a mandate ("make every effort to preserve the unity of the Spirit in the bond of peace"). God's plan for the integration of the whole creation in Christ is modelled in the ethnic reconciliation of God's new humanity. Such is the power of the gospel as promised to Abraham.[64]

#### The pax Romana and pax Christi

The Roman Empire was held together by swords and nails. The *pax Romana* was Rome's version of making peace by the blood of the cross—inflicting the cross on those who dared to resist. From a Roman prison Paul wrote about the *pax Christi*, the peace of Christ, peace on earth announced by angels to shepherds, God making peace by the blood of the cross[65]—the cross where Jesus died for sinners.

This new humanity, reconciled to God and to one another through the cross of Christ, is radically inclusive—making both Jews and Gentiles into citizens of God's people, members of God's family, and the place of God's dwelling.[66] God is not just up in heaven. God lives wherever his people allow God's image to be made again in them through Christ. We are called to make such unity visible and to be agents of the radical reconciliation that

---

[64] Ephesians 1:10; 2:1–16; 3:6; Galatians 3:6–8; see also Section IIF on the issue of unity and partnership within the Church.
[65] Colossians 1:20.
[66] Ephesians 2:19–22.

is at the heart of the gospel and is possible only in Christ. "Blessed are the peacemakers," said Jesus—a task that calls us to work, struggle, and suffer in a world of terrible conflicts.

We affirm that whereas the Jewish people were not strangers to the covenants and promises of God, in the way that Paul describes the Gentiles, they still stand in need of reconciliation to God through the Messiah Jesus. There is no difference, said Paul, between Jew and Gentile in sin; neither is there any difference in salvation. Only in and through the cross can both have access to God the Father through the one Spirit.[67]

A. *We continue, therefore, strongly to affirm the need for the whole Church to share the good news of Jesus as Messiah, Lord, and Saviour with Jewish people.* And in the spirit of Romans 14–15, we urge Gentile believers to accept, encourage, and pray for Messianic Jewish believers, in their witness among their own people.

Reconciliation to God and to one another is also the foundation and motivation for seeking the justice that God requires, without which, God says, there can be no peace. True and lasting reconciliation requires acknowledgment of past and present sin, repentance before God, confession to the injured one, and the seeking and receiving of forgiveness. It also includes commitment by the Church to seeking justice or reparation, where appropriate, for those who have been harmed by violence and oppression.

B. *We long to see the worldwide Church of Christ,* those who have been reconciled to God, living out our reconciliation with one another and committed to the task and struggle of biblical peace-making in the name of Christ.

## Overview questions

1. Read Colossians 1:19–20, Romans 5:1, Isaiah 53:5, Matthew 5:9, and Galatians 5:22–23. What do these passages tell us about the true meaning of peace? Why is it so fundamental to human flourishing? In your context, what are the main reasons for conflicts in society? Does the Christian community model peace and peace-making? If not, why not? What practical steps do you need to take toward the reconciliation and peace-making the Lord expects of us among Christians and in the wider society?

---

[67] Ephesians 2:11–22; Romans 3:23; Romans 10:12–13; Ephesians 2:18.

**Digging deeper**

2. Read Ephesians 2:11–18. Why was it so important in the early church to break down the dividing walls between Jews and Gentiles? On what grounds was that possible? How does that show the ongoing need of Jewish people to respond to the gospel of Jesus Christ? Pray for Messianic Jewish believers with thanksgiving, and pray for those who witness to Jews today.

3. Our world is deeply scarred by war, exploitation, hatred, and injustice of every kind. Most people groups, historically or in the present, have acted cruelly toward another group, or have experienced cruelty, or have both given and received injustice. What can your Christian community, and the global church, do to bring about repentance, forgiveness, and restitution, both on the local scale and on the global scale? What examples can you think of where Christians have pioneered peace-making or the righting of some great wrong? Do we have responsibility for the sins committed by previous generations?

# 2. Christ's peace in ethnic conflict

Ethnic diversity is the gift and plan of God in creation.[68] It has been spoiled by human sin and pride, resulting in confusion, strife, violence, and war among nations. However, ethnic diversity will be preserved in the new creation, when people from every nation, tribe, people, and language will gather as the redeemed people of God.[69] We confess that we often fail to take ethnic identity seriously and to value it as the Bible does, in creation and redemption. We fail to respect the ethnic identity of others and ignore the deep wounds that such long-term disrespect causes.

*A. We urge church pastors and leaders to teach biblical truth on ethnic diversity.* We must positively affirm the ethnic identity of all church members.

---

[68] Deuteronomy 32:8; Acts 17:26.
[69] Revelation 7:9; 21:3, where the text reads, "they will be his peoples" (plural).

But we must also show how our ethnic loyalties are flawed by sin and teach believers that all our ethnic identities are subordinate to our redeemed identity as the new humanity in Christ through the cross.

## The mission of God

The mission of God takes humanity from the nations scattered in judgment at the city of Babel to the nations gathered in redemption in the city of God, when the leaves of the tree of life (Genesis 2–3) will be for the healing of the nations.[70]

We affirm there is no other hope for peace in the land of modern Israel and its neighbours than the reconciling power of the gospel. When Israeli Jews and Palestinian Arabs can say to one another, "I love you in Jesus' name," the world will see the powerful reconciling work of the Good News.

Such reconciliation to God and to one another is also the foundation and motivation for seeking the justice that God requires, without which, God says, there can be no peace. True and lasting reconciliation requires acknowledgment of past and present sin, repentance before God, confession to the injured one, and the seeking and receiving of forgiveness. It also includes commitment by the church to seeking justice or reparation where appropriate for those who have been harmed by violence and oppression.

We acknowledge with grief and shame the complicity of Christians in some of the most destructive contexts of ethnic violence and oppression, and the lamentable silence of large parts of the Church when such conflicts take place. Such contexts include the history and legacy of racism and black slavery; the holocaust against Jews; apartheid; "ethnic cleansing"; inter-Christian sectarian violence; decimation of indigenous populations; inter-religious, political, and ethnic violence; Palestinian suffering; caste oppression; and tribal genocide. Christians who, by their action or inaction, add to the brokenness of the world, seriously undermine our witness to the gospel of peace. Therefore:

B. *For the sake of the gospel, we lament, and call for repentance where Christians have participated in ethnic violence, injustice, or oppression.* We also call for repentance for the many times Christians have been complicit in such evils by silence, apathy, or presumed neutrality, or by providing defective theological justification for these.

---

[70] Genesis 11; Revelation 22:2.

## Questions from Rwanda

The Rwandan genocide in 1994 raises acute questions for the Church in a country with almost 90% of the population as professing Christians.

What kind of gospel was it that had been received that was, or had become, so devoid of social and ethical transformational power?

Why were the church's evangelization, discipling, and devotional fervour so shallow that they left the blood of tribalism untouched by the water of baptism?

How can we reconcile the claim that Africa has the fastest-growing churches in world Christianity with the contradiction of tribal wars, ethnic conflicts, and even genocide?

Shallow evangelism, as Jesus warned in the parable of the seeds, produces fast but shallow growth that will not survive the heat.

*We should include (rather than avoid) teaching on the ethnic demands of Christian discipleship in contexts of tension and violence.* Unless the church explicitly teaches and warns believers about the ethnic implications of the Lordship of Christ, it will always be vulnerable to the scandal of having Christians involved in ethnic conflicts because their identity and prejudices have not been radically transformed and converted to Christ.

If the gospel is not deeply rooted in the context, challenging and transforming underlying worldviews and systems of injustice, then, when the evil day comes, Christian allegiance is discarded like an unwanted cloak and people revert to unregenerate loyalties and actions. Evangelizing without discipling, or revival without radical obedience to the commands of Christ, are not just deficient; they are dangerous.

We long for the day when the Church will be the world's most visibly shining model of ethnic reconciliation and its most active advocate for conflict resolution.

Such aspiration, rooted in the gospel, calls us to:

*C. Embrace the fullness of the reconciling power of the gospel and teach it accordingly.* This includes a full biblical understanding of the atonement: that Jesus not only bore our sin on the cross to reconcile us to God, but destroyed our enmity, to reconcile us to one another.

*D. Adopt the lifestyle of reconciliation.* In practical terms this is demonstrated when Christians:

1. forgive persecutors, while having courage to challenge injustice on behalf of others;

2. give aid and offer hospitality to neighbours "on the other side" of a conflict, taking initiatives to cross barriers to seek reconciliation;

3. continue to witness to Christ in violent contexts; and are willing to suffer, and even to die, rather than take part in acts of destruction or revenge;

4. engage in the long-term healing of wounds after conflict, making the Church a safe place of refuge and healing for all, including former enemies.

*E. Be a beacon and bearer of hope.* We bear witness to God who was in Christ reconciling the world to himself. It is solely in the name of Christ, and in the victory of his cross and resurrection, that we have authority to confront the demonic powers of evil that aggravate human conflict, and have power to minister his reconciling love and peace.

## Overview questions

1. Read Genesis 11:1–9, Deuteronomy 32:8, Acts 17:26, and Revelation 5:9–10. What do these passages teach us about the problems and the potential of our ethnic diversity? What is the ground for harmony between all the ethnic groups of the world? What can Christians do in the face of ethnic conflict that is caused by the clash between religions? How can Christians promote justice and peace, together with forgiveness and grace, between ethnic groups that are hostile to one another?

## Digging deeper

2. How can we celebrate our ethnic particularities and the parts of our culture which are precious to us, while celebrating even more that we are "one in Christ Jesus" across our ethnic distinctions? What might that look like in practice in our local churches? Are monocultural churches in multicultural communities a denial of the gospel? In your context, what needs to happen to demonstrate reconciliation among Christians across ethnic groups as a witness to the world? What will you do about it?

3. In your culture, are there tensions, hatred, discrimination, or injustice between different ethnic communities, tribes, or castes? What is the role of the church to resolve these problems in wider society beyond the church? What would justice look like?

4. Ethnic conflict sometimes occurs between groups who claim to be Christian, or by a "Christian" nation against another which may or may not be "Christian." How would you explain how this could happen? Why does it show an inadequate understanding of the gospel and what Christ has done in his death and resurrection? What needs to be changed in our evangelism, discipleship, and teaching to prevent such an outrage to God?

5. When you experience ill treatment on racial grounds, what should you do? If you are persecuted, what should you do? What should you not do?

# 3. Christ's peace for the poor and oppressed

The biblical foundation for our commitment to seeking justice and *shalom* for the oppressed and the poor, is summarized in "The Cape Town Confession of Faith" section 7c. On that basis, we long for more effective Christian action on:

### Slavery and human trafficking

There are more people all around the world in slavery today (an estimated 27 million) than 200 years ago when Wilberforce fought to abolish the transatlantic slave trade. In India alone there are an estimated 15 million bonded children. The caste system oppresses low-caste groups and excludes Dalits. But sadly the Christian Church itself is infected in many places with the same forms of discrimination. The concerted voice of the global Church must be raised in protest against what is in effect one of the world's oldest systems of slavery. But if such global advocacy is to have any authenticity, the Church must reject all inequality and discrimination within itself.

Migration on an unprecedented scale in today's world, for a variety of reasons, has led to human trafficking on every continent, the widespread enslavement of women and children in the sex trade, and the abuse of children through enforced labour or military conscription.

A. *Let us rise up as the Church worldwide to fight the evil of human trafficking, and to speak and act prophetically to "set the prisoners free."* This must include addressing the social, economic, and political factors that feed the trade. The world's slaves call out to the global Church of Christ, "Free our children. Free our women. Be our voice. Show us the new society that Jesus promised."

### Poverty

We embrace the witness of the whole Bible, as it shows us God's desire both for systemic economic justice and for personal compassion, respect, and generosity towards the poor and needy. We rejoice that this extensive biblical teaching has become more integrated into our mission strategy and practice, as it was for the early Church and the Apostle Paul.[71]

---

[71] Acts 4:32–37; Galatians 2:9–10; Romans 15:23–29; 2 Corinthians 8–9.

Accordingly, let us:

B. *Recognize the great opportunity that the Millennium Development Goals have presented for the local and global Church.* We call on churches to advocate for them before governments, and to participate in efforts to achieve them, such as the Micah Challenge.

C. *Have courage to declare that the world cannot address, let alone solve, the problem of poverty without also challenging excessive wealth and greed.* The gospel challenges the idolatry of rampant consumerism. We are called, as those who serve God and not mammon, to recognize that greed perpetuates poverty, and to renounce it. At the same time, we rejoice that the gospel includes the rich in its call to repentance, and invites them to join the fellowship of those transformed by forgiving grace.

## Seeking justice for the oppressed

"Be imitators of God," said Paul.[72] "God defends the cause of the fatherless and the widow, and loves the foreigner, giving him food and clothing."[73] "What does the LORD require of you? To act justly, and to love mercy and to walk humbly with your God."[74]

The law, the prophets, the Psalms, the Wisdom literature, the Gospels and Acts, and the epistles—all affirm God's desire for justice and mercy. The church needs to return to its New Testament roots, planted in Old Testament soil, by obeying this dimension of biblical revelation in our living and teaching, and in exercising a voice and influence in the public arena around such matters of major international concern.

Let us educate ourselves—our mission agencies, our theological training institutions, and Christian NGOs—in relation to the (1) biblical, (2) theological, (3) moral, and (4) missional foundations for action for the poor. Let us inform ourselves on practical and strategic issues, such as the contextual nature of poverty, and its root causes; the relative definitions of wealth and poverty; the interplay of wealth, poverty, and human trafficking.

---

[72] Ephesians 5:1.
[73] Deuteronomy 10:18.
[74] Micah 6:8.

## Overview questions

1. Read Deuteronomy 10:18, Micah 6:8, and Luke 1:52–55. Why do you think God is so especially concerned for the poor, the widow, the fatherless, and the foreigner? Does this mean that it is good to be poor and wrong to be rich? In what practical ways can our Christian community reflect the love of God expressed for those in need of protection, resources, and welcome? What generous actions can you take locally and globally, whether you have large or small resources?

## Digging deeper

2. In your culture, how does slavery show itself? Through sex trafficking? Through illegal immigrants enslaved by gang masters? Through sweat shops, with slave labour? Through social organisation, such as a caste system? What are the social, economic, political, and religious factors that make such enslavement possible? How could the local Christian community try to bring about some changes? How could the global church together engage in urgent advocacy amongst political and economic power holders?

3. Read Acts 4:32–37, Galatians 2:9–10, Romans 15:23–29, and 2 Corinthians 8–9. What do these passages teach us about generosity and sharing? In your context, how could you express the same communal love, and being generous whether out of poverty or out of riches? What are the barriers in your culture that prevent people being generous and instead encourage greed, covetousness, and selfishness?

4. In wealthy societies, there are usually pockets of poverty. Sometimes wealth, whether personal or national, is built on past or present exploitation of others. How can those of us who are wealthy build a more just society and

a more just global economy? Agree on some practical steps—and act on them!

5. Read the Micah Challenge Declaration (www.micahchallenge.org, then track through to the Declaration) or look up the Global Generosity Movement (http://generositymovement.org, a combined Lausanne and World Evangelical Alliance initiative). What could you personally, or your local church together, do in response?

6. In what ways can we be generous other than through money? What difference would it make in your society if Christians were generous in friendship, care for neighbours, time invested in local youth, or other activities?

## 4. Christ's peace for people with disabilities

People with disabilities form one of the largest minority groups in the world, estimated to exceed 600 million. The majority of these live in the least developed countries, and are among the poorest of the poor. Although physical or mental impairment is a part of their daily experience, most are also disabled by social attitudes, injustice, and lack of access to resources. Serving people with disabilities does not stop with medical care or social provision; it involves fighting alongside them, those who care for them and their families, for inclusion and equality, both in society and in the Church. God calls us to mutual friendship, respect, love, and justice.

*A. Let us rise up as Christians worldwide to reject cultural stereotypes,* for as the Apostle Paul commented, "we no longer regard anyone from a human point of view."[75] Made in the image of God, we all have gifts God can use in his service. We commit both to minister to people with disabilities, and to receive the ministry they have to give.

B. *We encourage church and mission leaders to think not only of mission among those with a disability,* but to recognize, affirm, and facilitate the missional calling of believers with disabilities themselves as part of the Body of Christ.

C. *We are grieved that so many people with disabilities are told that their impairment is due to personal sin, lack of faith, or unwillingness to be healed.* We deny that the Bible teaches this as a universal truth.[76] Such false teaching is pastorally insensitive and spiritually disabling; it adds the burden of guilt and frustrated hopes to the other barriers that people with disabilities face.

D. *We commit ourselves to make our churches places of inclusion and equality for people with disabilities* and to stand alongside them in resisting prejudice and in advocating for their needs in wider society.

## Overview questions

1. How does your culture regard people with physical disabilities and mental disabilities? What ideas do people have about the causes of disability? What provisions are made for those with disabilities, and by whom? Can you identify any provisions which are missing? What practical advocacy could you engage in? Read John 9:1–3 and Acts 3:1–10. What do these passages tell us about what is, and what is not, the cause of disability in these instances? What is, and what is not, the cause of healing in these instances?

---

[75] 2 Corinthians 5:16.
[76] John 9:1–3.

## Digging deeper

2. In your culture, what do Christians do to model an inclusive love and respect for those who have a disability? In what ways might people with different disabilities feel excluded from communal worship? What could your congregation or agency do to be more inclusive of those with disabilities? How could you actively enable such people to contribute their God-given gifts for the good of the whole group and encourage them in responsible mission?

3. How should we pastor those who despite much prayer do not experience healing of illness or disability? Which Scriptures would you turn to? How could you support people with disabilities (e.g., those who are blind or cannot walk) and their families to be able to cope better with everyday life, to access education, and to find work?

# 5. Christ's peace for people living with HIV

HIV and AIDS constitute a major crisis in many nations. Millions are infected with HIV, including many in our churches, and millions of children are orphaned by AIDS. God is calling us to show his deep love and compassion to all those infected and affected and to make every effort to save lives. We believe that the teachings and example of Jesus, as well as the transforming power of his cross and resurrection, are central to the holistic gospel response to HIV and AIDS that our world so urgently needs.

*A. We reject and denounce all condemnation, hostility, stigma, and discrimination against those living with HIV and AIDS.* Such things are a sin and a disgrace within the Body of Christ. All of us have sinned and fallen short of God's glory; we have been saved only by grace, and we should be slow to judge, quick to restore and forgive. We also recognize with grief and compassion that very many people become infected with HIV through no fault of their own, and often through caring for others.

B. *We long that all pastors should set an example of sexual chastity and faithfulness,* as Paul commanded, and teach clearly and often that marriage is the exclusive place for sexual union. This is needed not only because it is the clear teaching of the Bible, but also because the prevalence of concurrent sexual partnerships outside marriage is a major factor in the rapid spread of HIV in the most affected countries.

C. *Let us, as the Church worldwide, rise to this challenge in the name of Christ and in the power of the Holy Spirit.* Let us stand together with our brothers and sisters in areas hardest hit by HIV and AIDS, through practical support, compassionate care (including care of widows and orphans), social and political advocacy, education programmes (particularly those that empower women), and effective prevention strategies appropriate to the local context. We commit ourselves to such urgent and prophetic action as part of the integral mission of the Church.

## Overview questions

1. Across the globe, many millions of people, including millions of children, are infected with, or affected by, HIV-AIDS, causing immense suffering. How can the church show the love and compassion of Christ for those who suffer, both within and beyond the church community? What is the role of the church in helping halt the spread of this dreadful disease?

## Digging deeper

2. What are the main causes of the transmission of HIV? How can the church speak and act in regard to each of these? In particular, how can the church be more clear in its teaching about and demonstration of the God-given pattern of sexual activity exclusively within faithful marriage between one man and one woman? What are the particular challenges to that biblical design in your culture?

3. Many children are infected at birth, and children and adults may be infected through unsterilized needles or through caring for an AIDS sufferer. How can these people, along with widows and orphans, be supported, loved, and cared for? What education programmes or practical steps might change the infection rate? How can the hungry poor be fed?

4. Prostitution (often out of poverty), the sex trade especially affecting women and children, and the need for men to seek work for long periods away from home all contribute to the spread of HIV. How could each of these complex issues be addressed, by small achievable local initiatives as well as on a larger scale? How does the gospel speak to each of them?

5. How can we demonstrate love and care for HIV-AIDS sufferers in place of the fear and rejection that have too often been the case? In your context, how could you and your Christian community show welcome?

## 6. Christ's peace for his suffering creation

Our biblical mandate in relation to God's creation is provided in "The Cape Town Confession of Faith" section 7a. All human beings are to be stewards of the rich abundance of God's good creation. We are authorized to exercise godly dominion in using it for the sake of human welfare and needs, for example in farming, fishing, mining, energy generation, engineering, construction, trade, medicine. As we do so, we are also commanded to care for the earth and all its creatures, because the earth belongs to God, not to us. We do this for the sake of the Lord Jesus Christ who is the Creator, Owner, Sustainer, Redeemer, and Heir of All Creation.

We lament over the widespread abuse and destruction of the earth's resources, including its bio-diversity. Probably the most serious and urgent challenge faced by the physical world now is the threat of climate change. This will disproportionately affect those in poorer countries, for it is there that climate extremes will be most severe and where there is little capability to adapt to them. World poverty and climate change need to be addressed together and with equal urgency.

## Creation care

By the second half of this century, there could be hundreds of millions of environmental refugees whose homes are no longer habitable because of rising sea level, or gross flooding, or persistent drought. The plight of the poor in such areas will become very much worse.

For 200 years, the growth of wealth in developed countries has largely come through cheap energy from the burning of fossil fuels. Its effect on the world's climate had not been realized, nor had it been realized that the damage from this falls disproportionately on the world's poorest countries. But now we do know this. There is therefore an inescapable moral imperative for rich countries to avoid further damage by rapidly reducing their own carbon emissions and to share their wealth and skills with developing countries to enable them to adapt to climate change and build sustainable economies. Christians should be prominent among those pressing the moral case for these objectives.

Jesus warns us to be alert to the signs of the times. Climate change, warnings about the potential collapse of the global economy, and the global crisis related to oil shortage, and food and water shortages, may constitute such signs in our era. Signs, in biblical terms, are not paralysing predictions of an unavoidable future but warnings to change our ways, to repent and believe the gospel of the reign of God.

At a personal level, let us embrace the goodness, abundance, and the limits of God's creation. We do this best through a productive and responsible life of work, rest, cultivation, industry, trade, science and art, enjoyment of family and neighbours, hospitality, gratitude, and generosity.

We encourage Christians worldwide to:

A. *Adopt lifestyles that renounce habits of consumption* that are destructive or polluting;

B. *Exert legitimate means to persuade governments* to put moral imperatives above political expediency on issues of environmental destruction and potential climate change;

*C. Recognize and encourage the missional calling* both of (1) Christians who engage in the proper use of the earth's resources for human need and welfare through agriculture, industry, and medicine, and (2) Christians who engage in the protection and restoration of the earth's habitats and species through conservation and advocacy. Both share the same goal for both serve the same Creator, Provider, and Redeemer.

## Overview questions

1. In your culture, what are the chief evidences of and causes of degradation of the environment? In your culture, what are the actions that cause degradation, either to your context or to some other part of the world? What changes could the church try to bring about locally, and what changes could the global church advocate for together? What is your church doing to help? In what ways could living more simply contribute to a healthier world for all? Think of some concrete examples. Commit to some lifestyle changes.

## Digging deeper

2. If you live in a wealthy economy, what are some of the ways in which you personally or in communities together could reduce use of fossil fuels or use of chemicals? What could you do—even if it is expensive—to move to more sustainable living? If you live in a poor economy, what are the particular challenges? Even within the context of poverty, what could you do to move toward more sustainable living?

3. In the face of sharply rising world population, what changes need to happen to rebalance human flourishing and a healthy creation? What is the relationship between overpopulation in a region and famine and other tragedies? Should governments seek to balance population growth and resources? How could the church contribute to that debate?

4. Together with your own church, agree on an achievable project that would restore a local habitat to good health. What steps would you need to take between talking about it and achieving it? What would you need to do in order for the change to be permanent, not temporary?

5. Read Luke 12:13–21 and Colossians 3:5–14. What do these passages teach about the nature of greed and its consequences? In a world gripped with covetousness and consumerism, what changes do we need to make to live simply and generously instead? How do we teach these values to our children in a positive way? (Note, it is not only the wealthy who can be greedy and covetous!)

# IIC

# LIVING THE LOVE OF CHRIST AMONG PEOPLE OF OTHER FAITHS

## 1. "Love your neighbour as yourself" includes persons of other faiths

In view of the affirmations made in "The Cape Town Confession of Faith" section 7d, we respond to our high calling as disciples of Jesus Christ to see people of other faiths as our neighbours in the biblical sense. They are human beings created in God's image, whom God loves and for whose sins Christ died. We strive not only to see them as neighbours, but to obey Christ's teaching by being neighbours to them. We are called to be gentle, but not naïve; to be discerning and not gullible; to be alert to whatever threats we may face, but not ruled by fear.

We are called to share good news in evangelism, but not to engage in unworthy proselytizing. *Evangelism*, which includes persuasive rational argument following the example of the Apostle Paul, is "to make an honest and open statement of the gospel which leaves the hearers entirely free to make up their own minds about it. We wish to be sensitive to those of other faiths, and we reject any approach that seeks to force conversion on them."[77] *Proselytizing*, by contrast, is the attempt to compel others to become "one of us," to "accept our religion," or indeed to "join our denomination."

*A. We commit ourselves to be scrupulously ethical in all our evangelism.* Our witness is to be marked by "gentleness and respect, keeping a clear conscience."[78] We therefore reject any form of witness that is coercive, unethical, deceptive, or disrespectful.

---

[77] *The Manila Manifesto*, Section 12.
[78] 1 Peter 3:15–16; compare Acts 19:37.

*B. In the name of the God of love,* we repent of our failure to seek friendships with people of Muslim, Hindu, Buddhist, and other religious backgrounds. In the spirit of Jesus, we will take initiatives to show love, goodwill, and hospitality to them.

*C. In the name of the God of truth,* we (1) refuse to promote lies and caricatures about other faiths, and (2) denounce and resist the racist prejudice, hatred, and fear incited in popular media and political rhetoric.

*D. In the name of the God of peace,* we reject the path of violence and revenge in all our dealings with people of other faiths, even when violently attacked.

*E. We affirm the proper place for dialogue with people of other faiths,* just as Paul engaged in debate with Jews and Gentiles in the synagogue and public arenas. As a legitimate part of our Christian mission, such dialogue combines confidence in the uniqueness of Christ and in the truth of the gospel with respectful listening to others.

## Overview questions

1. Read Acts 17:22–34, Psalm 100, and 1 Peter 3:15–16. What do these passages tell us about the need to bear witness to those of other faiths and how to do it? Why is it so important not to be coercive (exert pressure unfairly or manipulate people's weaknesses)? What forms of interfaith activities do you think are helpful and practical for friendship building and peace-making, and what are not? How can we teach our children to love those of other faiths without surrendering faithfulness to the one and only true God?

## Digging deeper

2. In your community, what other faiths are represented? What kind of relationships do Christians have with people from those groups? If you live in a society where those of other faiths are in a minority, what special care do you need to take in relation to them? If you live in a society where Christians are in a minority, and especially where there is persecution, how can you fulfil Christ's command to love those who persecute you, and yet to bear witness to them?

3. Read Luke 10:25–37, the story of the Good Samaritan. How do you think Jesus' original hearers would have reacted, given that Jews and Samaritans were sworn enemies with very different religious beliefs? Read Acts 10, the story of Cornelius and Peter; note especially Acts 10:1–8, 28, 34–35, 44–48. Do these passages tell us that good works save? When we encounter those of other faiths who display compassion, generosity toward the poor, and fine moral characters, who perhaps put professing Christians to shame, how do we understand where they stand before God? How should we pray for them?

4. Many of the world's most troubled regions today are places where there is religious conflict. How can Christians, locally and globally, be peacemakers? For western Christians especially, whose governments are involved in wars in Muslim contexts, how can we obey the command to love and make peace instead?

## 2. The love of Christ calls us to suffer and sometimes to die for the gospel

Suffering may be necessary in our missionary engagement as witnesses to Christ, as it was for his apostles and the Old Testament prophets.[79] Being willing to suffer is an acid test for the genuineness of our mission. God can use suffering, persecution, and martyrdom to advance his mission. "Martyrdom is a form of witness which Christ has promised especially to honour."[80] Many Christians living in comfort and prosperity need to hear again the call of Christ to be willing to suffer for him. For many other believers live in the midst of such suffering as the cost of bearing witness to Jesus Christ in a hostile religious culture. They may have seen loved ones martyred, or endured torture or persecution because of their faithful obedience, yet continue to love those who have so harmed them.

A. We hear and remember with tears and prayer the testimonies of those who suffer for the gospel. We pray for grace and courage, along with them, to "love our enemies" as Christ commanded us. We pray that the gospel may bear fruit in places that are so hostile to its messengers. As we rightly grieve for those who suffer, we remember the infinite grief God feels over those who resist and reject his love, his gospel, and his servants. We long for them to repent and be forgiven and find the joy of being reconciled to God.

### Suffering for the gospel

The Gentiles were, in Paul's day, those whom we would now call people of other faiths. They worshipped other gods within a worldview very different from the faith of Old Testament Israel or the New Testament church. But through the cross of Christ God was bringing such people into unity in the church along with believing Jews, as heirs, members, and sharers together with Israel (Ephesians 3:6). Paul was willing to suffer for the sake of bearing witness to the saving love of God among people of other faiths. But he spoke of such suffering "for the sake of you Gentiles" (Ephesians 3:1, 13), not to evoke pity but as something that reflected the glory of the gospel. If God in his wisdom considered the goal of a multicultural church worth dying for, Paul considered it worth suffering for. He was willing to go to prison to show the world that "the unsearchable riches of Christ" were more precious than comfort, safety, or prosperity. The wisdom and glory of God and the gospel were displayed not in Paul's prosperity but in his pain.

---

[79] 2 Corinthians 12:9–10; 4:7–10.
[80] The Manila Manifesto, Section 12.

Indeed, he counted "the fellowship of sharing in his sufferings"[81] greater than any material or religious benefit.

Many of us in the church today need to repent of our compromise with a gospel of comfort and prosperity. We are called to submit again to the call of Christ and the apostles to be willing to suffer and die for the gospel and to love Christ's gospel more than life itself.

However, we recognize the difference between the suffering of persecution that God allows as the cost of our bearing witness to the cross and the suffering in the world that is inflicted by human evil, injustice, violence, hunger, disease, and disaster. We accept the first as the inevitable consequence of seeking to "live a godly life in Christ Jesus."[82] The second is a reality we cannot avoid so long as we are fallen human beings living in the fallen world of this age. But such suffering is an affront to the God of *shalom* who longs for human well-being. We are called upon to fight against such suffering with all God's strength and to "overcome evil with good," in every dimension of human life, physical, material, social, and spiritual.

## Overview questions

1. Read Matthew 16:24–26. What does denying yourself and taking up the cross daily look like in practice in your life and in your community? Why does that commitment need to be repeated constantly? In your context, what are the cultural and family factors that make obeying this teaching most difficult? Deep-level discipleship will usually be countercultural at best and inviting persecution at worst. How can we help one another to be faithful to Christ at every level of our lives, even when the consequences are painful? How can we ensure that our suffering truly is for Christ's sake, and not as the result of our being unpleasant?

---

[81] Philippians 3:10.
[82] 2 Timothy 3:12.

## Digging deeper

2.  How do we reconcile the Lord's call to us to suffer, and his promises to bless us? Why does whole-hearted discipleship, in commitment to the Lord and his gospel, lead to suffering as well as blessing? In particular, when we cross cultures, or share the gospel and the gospel life with those different from ourselves, or convert from a previous faith to follow Christ, why is suffering highly likely? Why as believers do we consider such suffering worthwhile? What inspires us to endure it?

3.  How can we avoid the pitfalls of sensationalism when speaking of persecution and martyrdom? Why does it matter? How can we ensure honesty and integrity when reporting such things? What reliable resources are there available in your context? Are there particular factors that make some Christians strong and steadfast under persecution, while others turn their back on the Lord? Take time to pray for the troubled areas of our world, where Christians are known to be suffering.

4.  Some suffering is a result of living in a fallen world and affects people of all religions. If Christians have the chance to leave for a safer, better life elsewhere, should they go, or should they stay and serve the community with the love of Christ? How would you counsel a Christian thinking about leaving a poor, unhealthy inner city for suburban comfort? Or a Christian hoping to emigrate, legally or illegally, to a more prosperous country? When is it right to stay—or deliberately to move into an area of greater suffering for the gospel's sake?

## 3. Love in action embodies and commends the gospel of grace

"We are the aroma of Christ."[83] Our calling is to live and serve among people of other faiths in a way that is so saturated with the fragrance of God's grace that they smell Christ, that they come to taste and see that God is good. By such embodied love, we are to make the gospel attractive in every cultural and religious setting. When Christians love people of other faiths through lives of love and acts of service, they embody the transforming grace of God.

### *Living out the power and wisdom of Christ*

Not only is the gospel to be preached to the Gentiles, but also the wisdom of God is proclaimed to all earthly and demonic powers. How? Through the church.[84] This is a people created by grace, whose very existence, as the new humanity redeemed from all nations but united in Christ, is proof of God's grace and the divine wisdom of the gospel. The church exists to demonstrate that grace of God in the life of sacrificial love. What the church does on earth is in itself a message preached, not just to people but also to principalities and powers. When Christians love people of other faiths through lives of love and acts of service, they embody the transforming grace of God among those to whom it is alien.

In cultures of "honour," where shame and vengeance are allied with religious legalism, "grace" is an alien concept. In these contexts, God's vulnerable, self-sacrificing love is not something to be debated; it is considered too foreign, even repulsive. Here, grace is an acquired taste, over a long time, in small doses, for those hungry enough to dare to taste it. The aroma of Christ gradually permeates all that his followers come into contact with.

*A. We long for God to raise up more men and women of grace* who will make long-term commitments to live, love, and serve in tough places dominated by other religions, to bring the smell and taste of the grace of Jesus Christ into cultures where it is unwelcome and dangerous to do so. This takes patience and endurance, sometimes for a whole life-time, sometimes unto death.

---

[83] 2 Corinthians 2:15.
[84] Ephesians 3:10.

## Overview questions

1. How does love in action demonstrate the grace of God? Why are visible, loving, and transformative acts of service, along with godly character, essential to the true communication of the gospel? How should this affect every part of our evangelism and church planting strategy? How will love in action affect the whole of our life, every day and in every sphere of life?

## Digging deeper

2. How would you explain "grace" to a Muslim, a Buddhist, a Hindu, and a secularist? What are the barriers for understanding grace for each of these? Why might love in action be more powerful than words in the first instance, or indeed for a long time?

3. Why is it so important that the Christian community together, not just an individual, demonstrates the transforming and transformative grace of Christ? How could you show this together? How does this work if you live in a context where to be a Christian, or to become a Christian, is illegal, or invites persecution?

4. Gather stories from your context of people whose lives have commended the gospel of grace. What was the effect of their testimony, lived and spoken? In your cultural style, compose a song that commemorates Christians of the past, with thanksgiving to God for them.

5. Why is it so hard to go to, and stay in, one of the tough places of the world for the sake of the gospel? What does the global church need to do together to reach the unreached, investing in the long-term commitment of gospel sowing, whether or not there is significant response for a very long time? What qualities of discipleship are needed, and how are they nurtured?

# 4. Love respects diversity of discipleship

So-called "insider movements" are to be found within several religions. These are groups of people who are now following Jesus as their God and Saviour. They meet together in small groups for fellowship, teaching, worship, and prayer centred around Jesus and the Bible while continuing to live socially and culturally within their birth communities, including some elements of its religious observance. This is a complex phenomenon and there is much disagreement over how to respond to it. Some commend such movements. Others warn of the danger of syncretism. Syncretism, however, is a danger found among Christians everywhere as we express our faith within our own cultures.

## Culture and the gospel

As in the New Testament, when Gentiles turned from the gods of their previous religions to trust in the living God and his Son Jesus Christ, so today many people are becoming followers of Jesus within cultures shaped by other world faiths. In the New Testament, this created challenges both for Gentile-background believers and Jewish-background believers. Similar tensions still trouble the church in mission today.

All believers have to make careful discernment as to what elements of any religious culture bear marks of God's common grace and providence (which we should welcome and bring under the Lordship of Christ), and what elements are idolatrous or demonic (which must be renounced and rejected as incompatible with our singular allegiance to Christ). Such discernment is primarily the responsibility of Christian believers in their own religio-cultural context, with the help of the Holy Spirit and the Scriptures, as the gospel takes root in their lived discipleship. It is not something to be decided for them or imposed upon them by outside experts. At the same time, the global body of Christ must be engaged in collective discernment and mutual correction in such areas. All of us need the eyes of others to see what is defective, dangerous, or compromised in the ways we have related our faith in Christ to the culture in which we live. We need to emulate the example of Barnabas, a Jewish believer who was commissioned to assess the first large-scale movement of Gentile-background believers in Antioch, who "when he saw the evidence of the grace of God, *he was glad* and encouraged them all to remain true to the Lord."[85] He then ensured that they were thoroughly discipled by good teaching.

We should avoid the tendency, when we see God at work in unexpected or unfamiliar ways, either (1) hastily to classify it and promote it as a new mission strategy, or (2) hastily to condemn it without sensitive contextual listening.

A. *In the spirit of Barnabas* who, on arrival in Antioch, "saw the evidence of the grace of God" and "was glad and encouraged them all to remain true to the Lord,"[86] we would appeal to all those who are concerned with this issue to:

1. Take as their primary guiding principle the apostolic decision and practice: "We should not make it difficult for the Gentiles who are turning to God."[87]

2. Exercise humility, patience, and graciousness in recognizing the diversity of viewpoints, and conduct conversations without stridency and mutual condemnation.[88]

## Overview questions

1. Read Acts 11:1–3, 13–18, and 19–24. Why is it difficult to discern God's hand in what is unfamiliar? What can we learn from these two stories? What principles do they give us for responding with discernment when we encounter those claiming to be believers but whose way of expressing their faith is very different from our own? When church planting, should we start a new congregation when there is already one in existence, although different from our own tradition and expressing their faith differently? Why? Why not?

---

[85] Acts 11:20–24.
[86] Acts 11:20–24.
[87] Acts 15:19.
[88] Romans 14:1–3.

## Digging deeper

2. When people from inside another religion come to faith in Christ, what principles should guide them in discerning what parts of their past life they can retain and what parts they must break away from? Is it possible for an outsider to decide? Why? Why not? What are the advantages, and what are the dangers, of staying as closely within the former community as possible?

3. Read Romans 12:1–2. How do Word and Spirit instruct a humble, dedicated disciple? Why is this an important instruction for all believers, whatever their circumstances, including those of us who live in cultures with a long history of Christian witness? How do we balance responsible contextualisation (incarnating the gospel in a culture) and radical obedience (letting God's Word pass judgment on our culture)?

4. Why do Christians, reading the same Bible, reach different conclusions about matters of belief and conduct? How should we handle disagreements? As the church becomes increasingly global in the grace of God, it also becomes increasingly diverse. Does that matter, or should we all look the same? How could different parts of God's family, united around the gospel, celebrate both unity and diversity, to the glory of God?

## 5. Love reaches out to scattered peoples

People are on the move as never before. Migration is one of the great global realities of our era. It is estimated that 200 million people are living outside their countries of origin, voluntarily or involuntarily. The term "diaspora" is used here to mean people who have relocated from their lands of birth for whatever reason. (The word "diaspora" meaning "a scattering" is used to describe this large-scale movement of people from their homeland to settle permanently or temporarily in other countries.)[89] **Vast numbers of people from many religious backgrounds, including Christians, live in diaspora conditions: economic migrants seeking work; internally-displaced peoples because of war or natural disaster; refugees and asylum seekers; victims of ethnic cleansing; people fleeing religious violence and persecution; famine sufferers—whether caused by drought, floods, or war; victims of rural poverty moving to cities.**

## Migrants in the biblical narrative and migrants now

*Permanent residents.* Those who become permanent residents in their host country may not have originally intended to stay. Some even become citizens.

*Temporary migrants* include, for example, international students; contract workers; business people; professionals and entrepreneurs; international bureaucrats and NGO workers; seamen; illegal immigrants; and military and diplomatic personnel.

*Displaced people* include refugees or asylum seekers, who may be either temporary or permanent.[90] Many arrive as Christian believers in cultures dominated by other faiths (e.g., Philippine workers in Gulf states) or in cultures of declining Christian allegiance (e.g., Africans and West Indians in the UK; Hispanics in the USA).

We find diaspora throughout the Bible. Cain moves to a life of homelessness. The ancestors of Israel leave their homes at God's command, for a life of pilgrimage. The people of Israel experience the life of famine as refugees in Egypt, of wandering in the wilderness, and later of being scattered in exile. The Son of Man, who in infancy found refuge in Egypt, had nowhere to lay his head and needed the hospitality of others. His followers are described as "aliens and strangers" in the world. Joseph, Daniel, and Esther exemplify believers seizing opportunities to serve God in exilic conditions. Ruth is a migrant who comes to faith in the God of her host family. Naaman is the foreign (enemy) visitor who finds the living God and then returns to his own land with a new faith that will face public and professional challenges. The Jewish diaspora, west and east, provided communities of expectant Jews and "God-fearer" Gentiles among whom the gospel spread. Migration has always been a factor in the expansion of the Christian faith: the scattering of Christians after the fall of Jerusalem;

---

[89] *Lausanne Occasional Paper #55.*

[90] *Lausanne Occasional Paper #55*: Diasporas & International Students: The New People Next Door.

the trade routes by land and sea from the Mediterranean to China, India, Afghanistan, and Arabia; European migrations from the early Middle Ages; the migration of millions from Europe to the Americas, Oceania, and Africa; reverse migration of former slaves back to Africa.

Believers who find themselves living in diaspora have unique opportunities to bear witness to their faith in the host community. Jeremiah told the exiles in Babylon to seek the *shalom* of that city and to pray to God for it.[91] It is possible that one of the keys to the renewal of the church in the west lies in the presence of many active, witnessing believers among the influx of migrant peoples. We therefore welcome the presence of living and growing migrant churches in the western world.

Believers in host communities that receive immigrants from non-Christian backgrounds have unique opportunities to bear witness to their faith, in word and deed, and to do it in their own neighbourhoods among people the church could never otherwise reach with the gospel. Such witness will stand in stark contrast to the prevailing climate of hostility, prejudice, and fear in many host cultures.

We are convinced that contemporary migrations are within the sovereign missional purpose of God, without ignoring the evil and suffering that can be involved.[92]

A. *We encourage Church and mission leaders* to recognize and respond to the missional opportunities presented by global migration and diaspora communities, in strategic planning, and in focused training and resourcing of those called to work among them.

B. *We encourage Christians in host nations* which have immigrant communities and international students and scholars of other religious backgrounds to bear counter-cultural witness to the love of Christ in deed and word, by obeying the extensive biblical commands to love the stranger, defend the cause of the foreigner, visit the prisoner, practise hospitality, build friendships, invite into our homes, and provide help and services.[93]

C. *We encourage Christians who are themselves part of diaspora communities* to discern the hand of God, even in circumstances they may not have chosen, and to seek whatever opportunities God provides for bearing witness to Christ in their host community and seeking its welfare.[94] Where that

---

[91] Jeremiah 29:7.
[92] Genesis 50:20.
[93] Leviticus 19:33–34; Deuteronomy 24:17; Ruth 2; Job 29:16; Matthew 25:35–36; Luke 10:25–37; 14:12–14; Romans 12:13; Hebrews 13:2–3; 1 Peter 4:9.
[94] Jeremiah 29:7.

host country includes Christian churches, we urge immigrant and indigenous churches together to listen and learn from one another, and to initiate co-operative efforts to reach all sections of their nation with the gospel.

## Overview questions

1. In the Bible, both Old and New Testaments, what are some of the different reasons why God's people migrated at different times in their history? How did God use these different circumstances? What basic lessons does that teach us for today? What movements can we see of those who were not at that time part of God's people? What can we learn from that? Why do people migrate today, either permanently or temporarily (e.g., as students)? How should we respond to the "scattered peoples" in our midst, whatever the reason for their migration?

## Digging deeper

2. In your culture, what are the causes of immigration and emigration (people coming in, people going out)? What problems—social, economic, emotional—result for the individual migrants, for the host society, and for the community left behind? What are the benefits to the society to which they go and to the society from which they come? Is the current level of migration sustainable and/or healthy? If so, why? If not, why not?

3. What specific opportunities are there for mission through migration movements or among international students and scholars? What special care should Christians show toward immigrants, and why? How could your Christian community be active in this? How can host country churches enable Christian immigrants and international students to serve the Lord fully in their new contexts? How can immigrant Christians reach out to unbelievers in the host country and not just retreat to a ghetto of their own culture?

4. What are the special problems of being homeless or stateless? Many of today's migrants are Christians, many are followers of other faiths, and most are fleeing war, poverty, and famine. Should we differentiate in how we show care and compassion toward them? What practical steps can we take to show love?

5. Find out about who are the migrants who have moved to your area. They may be internal migrants, displaced from one part of the country or tribal group to another, or they may have come from another country. Are they fleeing trouble or poverty, or are they coming voluntarily to study or work? Do any of these migrants come from people groups where there are very few Christians? What could you do to reach them with the love of God?

# 6. Love works for religious freedom for all people

## *Religious freedom*

Two thirds of humanity live in contexts where freedom of religious choice and expression is highly restricted either by government or through social pressure. As a result non-Christians are restricted in their freedom to become Christians if they wish to do so, and Christians along with people of other religions are restricted in their freedom "either alone or in community with others and in public or private, to manifest [their] religion or belief in teaching, practice, worship, and observance".[95]

Freedom of choice is a fundamental right of all human beings created in the image of God. We must resist violations of religious freedom wherever they exist. This is the nature of social and legal tolerance. The right to religious freedom is indivisible and cannot be claimed for one particular group only to the exclusion of others.

---

[95] United Nations Universal Declaration of Human Rights [UNDHR], Article 18.

Upholding human rights by defending religious freedom is not incompatible with following the way of the cross when confronted with persecution. There is no contradiction between being willing personally to suffer the abuse or loss of our own rights for the sake of Christ, and being committed to advocate and speak up for those who are voiceless under the violation of their human rights. We must also distinguish between advocating the rights of people of other faiths and endorsing the truth of their beliefs. We can defend the freedom of others to believe and practise their religion without accepting that religion as true.

A. *Let us strive for the goal of religious freedom for all people.* This requires advocacy before governments on behalf of Christians and people of other faiths who are persecuted.

B. *Let us conscientiously obey biblical teaching to be good citizens,* to seek the welfare of the nation where we live, to honour and pray for those in authority, to pay taxes, to do good, and to seek to live peaceful and quiet lives. The Christian is called to submit to the state, unless the state commands what God forbids, or prohibits what God commands. If the state thus forces us to choose between loyalty to itself and our higher loyalty to God, we must say No to the state because we have said Yes to Jesus Christ as Lord.[96]

In the midst of all our legitimate efforts for religious freedom for all people, the deepest longing of our hearts remains that all people should come to know the Lord Jesus Christ, freely put their faith in him and be saved, and enter the kingdom of God.

## Overview questions

1. Why is freedom such a precious part of human flourishing? Why is religious freedom so deeply resisted in some countries and people groups? Do those of us who have religious freedom fully appreciate our privilege? Do those of us who do not live under religious freedom use that as an excuse to not share the gospel? Read Daniel 1 and Daniel 3. What do we learn about faithfulness to God even when there is no freedom?

---

[96] Jeremiah 29:7; 1 Peter 2:13–17; 1 Timothy 2:1–2; Romans 13:1–7; Exodus 1:15–21; Daniel 6; Acts 3:19–20; 5:29.

## Digging deeper

2. Are human rights and religious freedom biblical values or western democratic and cultural values? Is it right to advocate for religious freedom for those who do not have it? If so, how should we engage in such advocacy? For those of us whose governments profess religious freedom, what restrictions are there in practice? How should we respond?

3. Why should Christians also defend the rights to religious freedom of those of other faiths? How might that be misunderstood? What should we do and say that maintains the uniqueness of Christ while also supporting universal religious freedom?

4. In what circumstances should Christians defy the laws of their country? In general, how can Christians commend the gospel through being good citizens? In what ways, in your community, could Christians bear witness to Christ through acts of service to all, whatever their religion?

5. Read Matthew 5:16, 1 Corinthians 10:31–11:1, and 1 Peter 2:11–17. What do these passages tell us about the appropriate use of freedom? What is the effect of "living good lives"? In your culture, what does that look like? Why does living a godly life sometimes lead to persecution?

# IID

# DISCERNING THE WILL OF CHRIST FOR WORLD EVANGELIZATION

## 1. Unreached and unengaged peoples

The heart of God longs that *all* people should have access to the knowledge of God's love and of his saving work through Jesus Christ. We recognize with grief and shame that there are thousands of people groups around the world for whom such access has not yet been made available through Christian witness. These are peoples who are *unreached*, in the sense that there are no known believers and no churches among them.[97] Many of these peoples are also *unengaged*, in the sense that we currently know of no churches or agencies that are even trying to share the gospel with them. Indeed, only a tiny percentage of the Church's resources (human and material) is being directed to the least-reached peoples. By definition these are peoples who will not invite us to come with the Good News, since they know nothing about it. Yet their presence among us in our world 2,000 years after Jesus commanded us to make disciples of all nations, constitutes not only a rebuke to our disobedience, not only a form of spiritual injustice, but also a silent "Macedonian Call."

*Reaching the unreached*

God is grieved wherever people do not know and love him, and we recognize that such people are found everywhere, including in the midst of nations that may have been evangelized generations or centuries ago. Nevertheless, there are whole communities where the gospel has never yet been heard even once, where the church has never existed.[98] It is urgent that we

---

[97] Ed: It is estimated that this may amount to 25% of the world's population.

[98] *The Joshua Project* defines an unreached or least-reached people as a people group among which there is no indigenous community of believing Christians with adequate numbers and resources to evangelize this people group.

ask: Why? How much longer must they wait? What will we do about it? It is estimated that 86% of people living in the context of major Muslim, Hindu, and Buddhist population blocks do not personally know any Christian.

While we celebrate the advance of the gospel in so many nations, we cannot rest while there are still so many peoples who have never heard. Like the shepherd in Jesus' story who left the ninety-nine sheep to seek the one that was lost, and like the Apostle Paul whose heart was set to reach those places where Christ had not been named, so we must continually assess the progress of world evangelization region by region and identify those who still wait to hear the good news of Jesus Christ.

Let us rise up as the Church worldwide to meet this challenge, and:

A. *Repent of our blindness* to the continuing presence of so many un-reached peoples in our world and our lack of urgency in sharing the gospel among them.

B. *Renew our commitment* to go to those who have not yet heard the gospel, to engage deeply with their language and culture, to live the gospel among them with incarnational love and sacrificial service, to communicate the light and truth of the Lord Jesus Christ in word and deed, awakening them through the Holy Spirit's power to the surprising grace of God.

C. *Aim to eradicate Bible poverty* in the world, for the Bible remains indispensable for evangelism. To do this we must:

1. Hasten the translation of the Bible into the languages of peoples who do not yet have any portion of God's Word in their mother tongue;

2. Make the message of the Bible widely available by oral means. (See also Oral cultures below.)

D. *Aim to eradicate Bible ignorance* in the Church, for the Bible remains indispensable for discipling believers into the likeness of Christ.

1. We long to see a fresh conviction, gripping all God's Church, of the central necessity of Bible teaching for the Church's growth in ministry, unity, and maturity.[99] We rejoice in the gifting of all those whom Christ has given to the Church as pastor-teachers. We will make every effort to identify, encourage, train, and support them in the preaching and teaching of God's Word. In doing so, however, we must reject the kind of clericalism that restricts the ministry

---

[99] Ephesians 4:11–12.

of God's Word to a few paid professionals, or to formal preaching in church pulpits. Many men and women, who are clearly gifted in pastoring and teaching God's people, exercise their gifting informally or without official denominational structures, but with the manifest blessing of God's Spirit. They too need to be recognized, encouraged, and equipped to rightly handle the Word of God.

2. We must promote Bible literacy among the generation that now relates primarily to digital communication rather than books, by encouraging digital methods of studying the Scriptures inductively with the depth of inquiry that at present requires paper, pens, and pencils.

*E. Let us keep evangelism at the centre* of the fully-integrated scope of all our mission, inasmuch as the gospel itself is the source, content, and authority of all biblically valid mission. All we do should be both an embodiment and a declaration of the love and grace of God and his saving work through Jesus Christ.

## Overview questions

1. Why do you think there are still so many people groups in the world where there is no known gospel witness? What needs to change in the global church together and your local congregation to change this situation? What practical steps could you personally take to raise awareness in your church or agency about unreached people groups and to encourage prayer and other action?

## Digging deeper

2. Why do you think most of the global church's resources, human and material, are applied to existing churches? In your own church or agency, what proportion of those resources, human and financial, are devoted to reaching those "outside," whether locally or far away? How can we foster a spirit of generosity, giving away both people gifts and money to bless others who as yet do not know the Lord?

3. How can we balance pioneering (going where the gospel has not been before, or into communities which urgently need re-evangelisation) and consolidating and maturing where the church already exists? What happens when pioneering is not followed by deep and ongoing discipling? Why does effective pioneering require long-term commitment? Many of the least reached peoples, especially where another religion is dominant, do not permit traditional Christian missionary work, so who may be best able to serve effectively in such a setting?

4. Read 2 Timothy 2:15 and 2 Timothy 3:12–17. Why is God's Word so fundamental in making disciples? Should all Christians be teachers of God's Word, or only professional pastor-teachers? How can they complement each other? In your context, how are pastor-teachers identified, trained, and then supported? Are they encouraged to be both mission focused (looking to reach the unreached and to teach mission) as well as pastorally focused (caring for those who are already believers)? Are there changes that need to happen? How can we all read all of Scripture, or hear it, with missionary eyes and ears?

5. Do you have the whole Bible in your mother tongue? Some of us have access to many translations and many resources for understanding the Bible, while some people groups have little or no Scripture in their own language as yet. How can we address this imbalance? Is it right to devote considerable resources to translating Scripture into a language used by only a few thousand people? (By no means all people groups without Scripture are that small!) Pause and pray for those involved in translation today.

6. In what ways does the digital revolution serve mission, including among unreached people groups? What are the potential gains, and what are the dangers, of disseminating Scripture in very small pieces? Is this any different from using tracts (small gospel leaflets) or sharing the gospel from a small selection of Bible texts? How can we use all these media, and many others, better in future?

# 2. Oral cultures

The majority of the world's population are oral communicators, who cannot or do not learn through literate means, and more than half of them are among the unreached as defined above. Among these, there are an estimated 350 million people without a single verse of Scripture in their language. In addition to the "primary oral learners" there are many "secondary oral learners," that is those who are technically literate but prefer now to communicate in an oral manner, with the rise of visual learning and the dominance of images in communication.

## Oral learners

It is estimated that 4,350,000,000 people in the world cannot or do not learn through literate means. We have a responsibility to tell God's Story in relevant ways, in mother tongue translation, and with respect for the recipients' learning preference. We believe that appropriate oral strategies will bear fruit in church planting and nurturing in such cultures. We affirm that such oral strategies are consistent with the Amsterdam 2000 Declaration:

We must proclaim and disseminate the Holy Scriptures in the heart language of all those we are called to evangelize and disciple, in written form and for oral learners.

As we recognize and take action on issues of orality, let us:

A. *Make greater use of oral methodologies* in discipling programmes, even among literate believers.

B. *Make available an oral format Story Bible* in the heart languages of unreached and unengaged people groups as a matter of priority.

C. *Encourage mission agencies to develop oral strategies,* including: the recording and distribution of oral Bible stories for evangelism, discipling, and leadership training, along with appropriate orality training for pioneer evangelists and church-planters; these could use fruitful oral and visual communication methods for communicating the whole biblical story of salvation, including storytelling, dances, arts, poetry, chants, and dramas.

D. *Encourage local churches in the Global South to engage with unreached people groups* in their area through oral methods that are specific to their worldview.

E. *Encourage seminaries to provide curricula that will train pastors and missionaries in oral methodologies.*

## Overview questions

1. In your culture, how do people prefer to communicate? Do you use different forms of communication (written, oral) for different purposes? For those who are able to read, do they have access to written resources, including the Bible, and, if so, do they read? If not, why not? For those where literacy levels are low, or books scarce or expensive, how does that shape the methods by which you teach and learn God's Word? Most of the believers in the early church were oral learners. How should that instruct and encourage us?

## Digging deeper

2. How have television and films changed preferred communication media in traditionally print-focused societies? What does the church need to do to respond to this change, both in evangelism and among those already believing? Why has "the Jesus film" been so effective in many societies, both literate and non-literate? How could this model be developed for further extensive Bible teaching? How do we reconcile faithfulness to the biblical text and the imagination and extra bits that are inevitable in turning material into a film?

3. In your agency, how do you encourage creative communication of biblical truth among oral learners? How much financial investment do you make in suitable resources? How could we develop better partnerships between churches, agencies, those engaged in radio ministry, those producing oral Bible story materials, and other agencies or groups?

4. In your culture, or in the culture where you serve if different, what are the traditional art forms (e.g., dance, drama, poetry, painting, music)? How can you harness these for gospel communication and for teaching and training believers? What principles would you use to set boundaries for adopting and adapting these forms? Why do you think Christians often remember hymns and Christian songs more easily than they memorise Scripture or recall a sermon? What should we learn from that?

# 3. Christ-centred leaders

The rapid growth of the Church in so many places remains shallow and vulnerable, partly because of the lack of discipled leaders, and partly because so many use their positions for worldly power, arrogant status, or personal enrichment. As a result, God's people suffer, Christ is dishonoured, and gospel mission is undermined. "Leadership training" is the commonly-proposed priority solution. Indeed, leadership training programmes of all kinds have multiplied, but the problem remains, for two probable reasons.

*First*, training leaders to be godly and Christ-like is the wrong way round. Biblically, only those whose lives already display basic qualities of mature discipleship should be appointed to leadership in the first place.[100] If, today, we are faced with many people in leadership who have scarcely been discipled, then there is no option but to include such basic discipling in their leadership development. Arguably the scale of un-Christ-like and worldly leadership in the global Church today is glaring evidence of generations of reductionist evangelism, neglected discipling, and shallow growth.

---

[100] 1 Timothy 3:1–13; Titus 1:6–9; 1 Peter 5:1–3.

The answer to leadership failure is not just more *leadership* training but better *discipleship* training. Leaders must first be disciples of Christ himself.

*Second*, some leadership training programmes focus on packaged knowledge, techniques, and skills to the neglect of godly character. By contrast, authentic Christian leaders must be like Christ in having a servant heart, humility, integrity, purity, lack of greed, prayerfulness, dependence on God's Spirit, and a deep love for people. Furthermore, some leadership training programmes lack specific training in the one key skill that Paul includes in his list of qualifications—ability to teach God's Word to God's people. Yet Bible teaching is the paramount means of disciple-making and the most serious deficiency in contemporary Church leaders.

### Biblical leadership

God's people need leaders. But the Bible shows that leaders can be as much the problem as the solution. Old Testament Israel strayed from God repeatedly, and bad leadership was the repeated root cause: arrogant kings, false prophets, corrupt priests. Godly leaders were few and exceptional in Israel. This was why God stepped in as promised, in Christ, to be the true, faithful leader of his people. Christian leadership must now reflect the character of our one Good Shepherd, the Lord Jesus. Sadly, the history of the Christian church has demonstrated the same tendency as Old Testament Israel.

The clear warning by Jesus to the first leaders of his church that the world's way of leadership "shall not be so among you," is ignored and disobeyed.[101]

Those entrusted with oversight and eldership must be tested as to their lives and character as mature disciples.[102] But we should not have to train leaders to conduct themselves in a godly manner. The need to do so at the leadership level highlights the prior failure at the discipling level. Let us make and train disciples, and let God call some trained disciples to be leaders.

A. *We long to see greatly intensified efforts in disciple-making,* through the long-term work of teaching and nurturing new believers, so that those whom God calls and gives to the Church as leaders are qualified according to biblical criteria of maturity and servanthood.

---

[101] Luke 22:24–27.
[102] 1 Timothy 3:1–13; Titus 1:6–9; 1 Peter 5:1–3.

*B. We renew our commitment to pray for our leaders.* We long that God would multiply, protect, and encourage leaders who are biblically faithful and obedient. We pray that God would rebuke, remove, or bring to repentance leaders who dishonour his name and discredit the gospel. And we pray that God would raise up a new generation of discipled servant-leaders whose passion is above all else to know Christ and be like him.

*C. Those of us who are in Christian leadership need to recognize our vulnerability* and accept the gift of accountability within the body of Christ. We commend the practice of submitting to an accountability group.

*D. We strongly encourage seminaries,* and all those who deliver leadership training programmes, to focus more on spiritual and character formation, not only on imparting knowledge or grading performance, and we heartily rejoice in those that already do so as part of comprehensive "whole person" leadership development.

## Overview questions

1. Read 2 Kings 15:1–4, 8–9, 17–18, 32–35 and 2 Kings 18:1–8. What do we learn about godly and ungodly leaders? What was the effect on the people? Why is leadership a solemn responsibility? Read Luke 22:24–27, 1 Timothy 3:1–13, and 1 Peter 5:1–6. What do these passages teach us about the character of a Christian leader and the task and role of a godly leader? How can we nurture our leaders so that being Christ-centred is the most important reality for them?

## Digging deeper

2. In many cultures, leadership is often inherited through one family or related to social status or wealth, to power, or perhaps to levels of education. How should Christian leaders be appointed in such contexts? Do any of these cultural factors matter? Why is servant leadership usually countercultural?

3. What are the best ways to train pastors and other Christian leaders? What is helpful in current training models in your culture, and what needs to be changed? In particular, what are the best ways in your context to train people in in-depth discipleship and in skilful understanding and teaching of God's Word?

4. If you are a leader, to whom are you accountable (besides the Lord)? How does that work in practice? What do you especially need to do to resist temptation and sin and to nurture integrity and ongoing closeness to the Lord?

5. What should church and agency members do to support and encourage their leaders in their God-given responsibilities? How are our expectations of our leaders often shaped by culture rather than by biblical principles? What should we do when we disagree with our appointed leaders and in the event of a leader failing through sin or incompetence?

# 4. Cities

Cities are crucially important for the human future and for world mission. Half the world now lives in cities. Cities are where four major kinds of people are most to be found: (1) the next generation of young people; (2) the most unreached peoples who have migrated; (3) the culture shapers; (4) the poorest of the poor.

A. *We discern the sovereign hand of God in the massive rise of urbanization in our time,* and we urge Church and mission leaders worldwide to respond to this fact by giving urgent strategic attention to urban mission. We must love our cities as God does, with holy discernment and Christ-like compassion, and obey his command to "seek the welfare of the city," wherever that may be. We will seek to learn appropriate and flexible methods of mission that respond to urban realities.

## Evangelization of cities

The Bible shows God's concern for cities. They can be targets of his judgment for their sin (Sodom and Gomorrah), or spared his judgment through repentance (Nineveh). The city can be the place of God's redemptive covenant presence, though that in itself does not spare the city from God's moral judgment and destruction (Jerusalem). The city is not only the pinnacle of human achievement, positively and negatively, but also the goal of God's redemptive work as the new creation is described as the eternal city of God in which God will dwell with his people forever.

One hundred of the world's major cities drive 30% of the world's economy and almost all of its innovation. The population shift to cities reminds us of God's love for the 120,000 people in Nineveh. Since human beings are made in the image of God, there is more image of God per square mile in cities than anywhere else on the planet.

Commitment to mission in the city will include the following imperatives. To:

1. Recognize that cities need contextually relevant mission approaches, not the importing of non-urban models of church and mission.

2. Be patient and sensitive in the midst of the multicultural tensions of urban life that will surface in any city church

3. Integrate Christian faith with daily work in the public arena and all its stresses and opportunities

4. Be open to rapid change, diversity, and disorder.

5. Combine intensely relevant evangelism with passionate advocacy and action in social compassion and justice on behalf of the poor and marginalized

6. Engage the world of the arts and media

7. Co-operate with many churches and agencies, across denominational and theological lines, in forming dynamic city-reaching movements.

## Overview questions

1. It is often said that God's revelation begins in a garden (Genesis 2:8) and ends in a city (Revelation 21). Read Revelation 21. What are the characteristics of this perfect city? How does this contrast with cities in your context, and others that you know about? In the book of Acts, why do the apostles so often base their ministry in cities? What are the specific opportunities that cities offer for spreading the gospel, and what are the most challenging factors? What draws people to cities? What makes people want to escape the city?

## Digging deeper

2. What changes do we need to make in our traditional patterns of evangelism in response to rapid urbanisation, in wealthy contexts and in contexts of poverty and deprivation? How can the church establish compassionate, meaningful communities in a city? Why do Roman Catholics and Pentecostals often work more effectively in poor urban areas than most Protestants, many evangelicals included? What can we all learn?

3. Why are cities often the starting point of riots and revolutions? How can Christian communities address some of the problems that give rise to these events? How can Christian professionals (architects, politicians, teachers, business people) contribute to well-being and justice in a city through their daily work?

4. Cities often bring people of different ethnic backgrounds and religions to live close to one another geographically, but commonly without any meaningful shared life. What is the special responsibility of Christians in such a setting? Often churches in a city live independently of one another. What must we do to create strong partnerships so that there can be greater impact for the gospel in our cities?

# 5. Children

*All* children are at risk. There are about two billion children in our world, and half of them are at risk from poverty. Millions are at risk from prosperity. Children of the wealthy and secure have everything to live with, but nothing to live for.

Children and young people are the Church of today, not merely of tomorrow. Young people have great potential as active agents in God's mission. They represent an enormous under-used pool of influencers with sensitivity to the voice of God and a willingness to respond to him. We rejoice in the excellent ministries that serve among and with children, and long for such work to be multiplied since the need is so great. As we see in the Bible, God can and does use children and young people—their prayers, their insights, their words, their initiatives—in changing hearts. They represent "new energy" to transform the world. Let us listen and not stifle their childlike spirituality with our adult rationalistic approaches.

We commit ourselves to:

A. *Take children seriously,* through fresh biblical and theological enquiry that reflects on God's love and purpose for them and through them, and by rediscovering the profound significance for theology and mission of Jesus' provocative action in placing "a child in the midst."[103]

B. *Seek to train people and provide resources to meet the needs of children worldwide,* wherever possible working with their families and communities, in the conviction that holistic ministry to and through each next generation of children and young people is a vital component of world mission.

---

[103] Mark 9:33–37.

*C. Expose, resist, and take action against all abuse of children,* including violence, exploitation, slavery, trafficking, prostitution, gender and ethnic discrimination, commercial targeting, and wilful neglect.

## Evangelization of children

There are no unreached children and youth. If the church does not reach them, someone will—other faiths, political ideologies, secularism, consumerism, corporate marketing, people traffickers, or many other unwholesome possibilities. Children and youth bear the brunt of our world's brokenness, and the worst aspects of globalization. And yet they are the most receptive generation to the truths of the gospel. Childhood and youth are when most decisions are made to follow Christ. Children are the shape of things to come. Either we help to shape their lives in godly ways, or the world will shape them into its own mould. Their minds and lives are filled with an unimaginable wealth of information, but no undeniable truths; nothing which provides meaning or purpose.

The covenant God of the Bible is the God of the generations. An abundance of under-explored Biblical material demonstrates God's concern for each next generation. But we acknowledge with grief that families and churches have often not passed the torch of faith to their children. By failing to reach the next generation, not only our children, but our churches and societies are at risk. We have not properly appreciated the contribution children can make in church and society. We are allowing a precious resource to slip through our fingers.

## Overview questions

1. Read Mark 9:33–37 and Mark 10:13–16. What do these passages teach us about Jesus' attitude toward children? Is that the way our churches treat children today? What do these passages teach us about Jesus' attitude to adults? What do we need to learn? With world population growing rapidly, what strategies do we need to develop to reach so many children with the gospel, without manipulation but while they are still developing life patterns? Is it ethical to try to disciple children if their parents are of another religion or none? What principles should guide us in such a situation?

## Digging deeper

2. In your culture, who or what (e.g., media, consumerism) shape children most of all? How should we disciple children most effectively? What special challenges are there if, like adults, children are called to be "in the world, but not of the world"? What are the reasons for, and the reasons against, trying to keep them in a wholly Christian environment during childhood?

3. In what ways can believing children contribute to the life of the church, including in worship services and in outreach? How should we teach them to pray and learn lessons from Scripture? How should we encourage them to witness to the Lord Jesus in their everyday lives, among their friends and schoolmates? As they grow, how can we help them to mature in their faith and to deal with intellectual and moral challenges?

4. Why do many children, brought up in Christian homes, turn their back on the faith as young people or in early adulthood? How can we do a better job of passing on the baton of faith to the next generation? Why is that such a vital responsibility? How can we support believing parents and grandparents in their vital role?

5. How can we care better for vulnerable children, and act against the tide of abuse, child trafficking, and child prostitution? Should we buy goods made through child labour? Why—and why not? There are often complex cultural factors involved in the greater rate of abortion of girl babies in some societies; how should the church respond? In your context, which are the children who are especially vulnerable, and in what ways? What could the Christian community do to care for them?

# 6. Prayer

In the midst of all these priorities, let us commit ourselves afresh to pray. Prayer is a call, a command, and a gift. Prayer is the indispensible foundation and resource for all elements of our mission.

*A. We will pray with unity, focus, persistence, and biblically-informed clarity:*

1. For God to send labourers into every corner of the world, in the power of his Spirit;

2. For the lost in every people and place to be drawn to God by his Spirit, through the declaration of the truth of the gospel and the demonstration of Christ's love and power;

3. For God's glory to be revealed and Christ's name to be known and praised because of the character, deeds, and words of his people. We will cry out for our brothers and sisters who suffer for the name of Christ;

4. For God's kingdom to come, that God's will may be done on earth as in heaven, in the establishment of justice, the steward-ship and care of creation, and the blessing of God's peace in our communities.

*B. We will continually give thanks as we see God's work among the nations,* looking forward to the day when the kingdom of this world will become the kingdom of our God and of his Christ.

## Overview questions

1. Read Matthew 6:5–15; 9:35–38; Acts 4:23–31; and 2 Corinthians 4:1–7. What do these passages teach us about why prayer is so important, how we are to pray, and what we are to pray about? In relation to evangelism in particular, why do we need to pray?

## Digging deeper

2. Why is it easier to talk about prayer than in fact to pray? Read Romans 8:26–27 and Hebrews 5:14–16; 10:19–25. What wonderful motivations do these passages hold out to us to pray?

3. Paul tells us to "pray without ceasing" or "continually" (1 Thessalonians 5:17). How in practise can we weave prayer into every waking moment, whatever we are doing, and not just in prayer meetings or times of personal devotions? How can we "practise the presence of Christ"? How can we encourage one another to pray in this way?

4. What does it mean "to pray in faith," either in relation to our circumstances, or to desire for healing, or when we long for the salvation of those as yet unsaved? What does it not mean? How will we recognise what God is doing, even when his answer is different from what we might have prayed for and hoped for? Share testimonies of God's response to prayers, both when he grants what you have asked for and when he hasn't. What are the special challenges of both?

5. In the light of so many as yet unreached people groups, close at hand or far away, how could you and your Christian community pray more meaningfully for at least some of them? What resources do you have access to, to provide information? Why does fervent, constant prayer often lead to other action as well?

# IIE

## CALLING THE CHURCH OF CHRIST BACK TO HUMILITY, INTEGRITY, AND SIMPLICITY

Walking is the biblical metaphor for our way of life and daily conduct. Seven times in Ephesians Paul speaks of how Christians should, or should not, walk.[104]

## 1. Walk in distinctiveness, as God's new humanity[105]

The people of God either walk in the way of the Lord, or walk in the ways of other gods. The Bible shows that God's greatest problem is not just with the nations of the world, but with the people he has created and called to be the means of blessing the nations. And the biggest obstacle to fulfilling that mission is idolatry among God's own people. For if we are called to bring the nations to worship the only true and living God, we fail miserably if we ourselves are running after the false gods of the people around us.

When there is no distinction in conduct between Christians and non-Christians—for example in the practice of corruption and greed, or sexual promiscuity, or rate of divorce, or relapse to pre-Christian religious practice, or attitudes towards people of other races, or consumerist lifestyles, or social prejudice—then the world is right to wonder if our Christianity makes any difference at all. Our message carries no authenticity to a watching world.

---

[104] Though translated variously, the following texts all use the verb "to walk": Ephesians 2:2; 2:10; 4:1; 4:17; 5:2; 5:8; 5:15.

[105] Ephesians 4:16–31.

*A. We challenge one another, as God's people* in every culture, to face up to the extent to which, consciously or unconsciously, we are caught up in the idolatries of our surrounding culture. We pray for prophetic discernment to identify and expose such false gods and their presence within the Church itself, and for the courage to repent and renounce them in the name and authority of Jesus as Lord.

*B. Since there is no biblical mission without biblical living, we urgently recommit ourselves,* and challenge all those who profess the name of Christ, to live in radical distinctiveness from the ways of the world, to "put on the new humanity, created to be like God in true righteousness and holiness."

## Overview questions

1. Read Ephesians 4:15–32. What does this passage teach us about the difference there should be between Christians and unbelievers? Is that the way people who are not Christian see your Christian community? If not, why not? Are there specific areas where Christians conform to cultural norms in your society rather than to Scripture? How should Christian discipline and Christian compassion come together in particular instances? How can a Christian community be winsome and attractive in its discipleship?

## Digging deeper

2. Why do we find it so difficult to see the truth about our own behaviour? How can we help one another be more discerning about the transformation God looks for, and for which he promises adequate resources? How can the different parts of the world church speak with humility to other parts, for mutual blessing and God's glory? What are the barriers to hearing?

3. Paul is realistic in Romans 7:14–25 about the struggle against sin that a believer can experience. What have been some of your experiences of such struggles? How should we deal pastorally with those who fail in some way? What should we do? What should we not do?

4. Why is the way Christians conduct themselves so crucial for effective evangelism? In your society, what are the things which unbelievers find most offensive about Christians? Are these inevitable stumbling blocks, or are they things for which we must repent and learn to walk differently in future? What practical actions do you need to take?

## 2. Walk in love, rejecting the idolatry of disordered sexuality[106]

God's design in creation is that marriage is constituted by the committed, faithful relationship between one man and one woman, in which they become one flesh in a new social unity that is distinct from their birth families, and that sexual intercourse as the expression of that "one flesh" is to be enjoyed exclusively within the bond of marriage. This loving sexual union within marriage, in which "two become one," reflects both Christ's relationship with the Church and also the unity of Jew and Gentile in the new humanity.[107]

Paul contrasts the purity of God's love with the ugliness of counterfeit love that masquerades in disordered sexuality and all that goes along with it. Disordered sexuality of all kinds, in any practice of sexual intimacy before or outside marriage as biblically defined, is out of line with God's will and a parody of his blessing. The abuse and idolatry that surround disordered sexuality contribute to wider social decline, including the breakdown of marriages and families and produce incalculable suffering of loneliness and exploitation. Disordered sexuality is a serious issue within the Church itself, and it is a tragically common cause of leadership failure.

---

[106] Ephesians 5:1–7.
[107] Ephesians 5:31; 2:15.

## Christ's model for us

To be like God is above all to imitate his self-sacrificial love, modelled perfectly in Christ's love for us. Such love requires of us kindness, compassion, and forgiveness. "For the sake of the glory of God and the evangelization of the world, nothing is more important than that the church should be, and should be seen to be, God's new society."[108]

We recognize our need for deep humility and consciousness of failure in this area. We long to see Christians challenging our surrounding cultures by living according to the standards to which the Bible calls us.

*A. We strongly encourage all pastors:*

1. To facilitate more open conversation about sexuality in our churches, declaring positively the good news of God's plan for healthy relationships and family life, but also addressing with pastoral honesty the areas where Christians share in the broken and dysfunctional realities of their surrounding culture;

2. To teach God's standards clearly, but to do so with Christ's pastoral compassion for sinners, recognising how vulnerable we all are to sexual temptation and sin;

3. To strive to set a positive example in living by biblical standards of sexual faithfulness;

*B. As members of the Church we commit ourselves:*

1. To do all we can in the Church and in society to strengthen faithful marriages and healthy family life;

2. To recognize the presence and contribution of those who are single, widowed, or childless, to ensure the church is a welcoming and sustaining family in Christ, and to enable them to exercise their gifts in the full range of the church's ministries;

3. To resist the multiple forms of disordered sexuality in our surrounding cultures, including pornography, adultery, and promiscuity;

4. To seek to understand and address the deep heart issues of identity and experience which draw some people into homosexual practice; to reach out with the love, compassion and justice of Christ, and to reject and condemn all forms of hatred, verbal or physical abuse, and victimization of homosexual people;

---

[108] John Stott, *The Message of Ephesians* (Leicester: Inter-Varsity Press, 1979), 10.

5. To remember that by God's redemptive grace no person or situation is beyond the possibility of change and restoration.

## Overview questions

1. Read Genesis 2:20–25, Ephesians 5:21–33, and 1 Corinthians 13:1–13. What do these passages teach us about the nature of love and about the relationship within marriage of a man and a woman? How do we live up to such high standards? How can we strengthen marriages so that more are loving and faithful according to God's design? How can we disciple our children and young people so that they are able to resist engaging in sexual activity outside of God's design and positively value God's pattern?

## Digging deeper

2. In your context, what are the main challenges to the biblical standards for sexual expression? How does your culture's understanding of love differ from the Bible's? Why does the Bible say so much about sex? Why is faithful monogamy (one sexual partner, of the opposite gender, and for life) so contested in so many cultures? Why do Christian leaders so often fail in this area? What needs to happen to protect them from temptation and sin?

3. How should we deal pastorally with those converted after ungodly sexual behaviour (e.g., premarital promiscuity, adultery), and those who sin after becoming professing Christians? When should the church exercise discipline, and what form should that take? How should the church care for children and innocent spouses following relationship breakdown? How should the church strengthen God's standards for sexual expression for all its members, including those who are unmarried or widowed?

4. What draws people into homosexuality? How should the church respond to practising homosexuals who seek membership, in a way which does not reject or alienate? Does your church have a consistent attitude toward practising homosexuals, men and women living together outside marriage, and those who have engaged in adultery?

5. In your context, what are the main factors that have led to the tragic spread of sexual diseases? How can the church show the love of God to those affected, either through their own fault or (as is often the case) through no fault of their own? Social, economic, and cultural factors can be very complex as they affect sexual behaviour, and poverty and famine contribute to a high death rate in some places. What is the role of the global church to address some of these issues, in loving partnership with local Christians? How can the church support widows and orphans?

# 3. Walk in humility, rejecting the idolatry of power[109]

In our fallenness and sin, power is often exercised to abuse and exploit others. We exalt ourselves, claiming superiority of gender, race, or social status. Paul counters all these marks of the idolatry of pride and power with his requirement that those who are filled by God's Spirit should submit to one another for Christ's sake. Such mutual submission and reciprocal love is to be expressed in marriage, family, and socio-economic relations.

A. *We long to see all Christian husbands and wives, parents and children, employers and employees, living out the Bible's teaching* about "submitting to one another out of reverence for Christ."

B. *We encourage pastors to help believers* understand, honestly discuss, and practise the mutual submission that God requires of his children towards one another. In a world of greed, power, and abuse, God is calling his Church to be the place of gentle humility and selfless love among its members.

---

[109] Ephesians 5:15–6:4.

C. *We particularly and urgently call Christian husbands to observe the balance of responsibilities in Paul's teaching about husbands and wives.* Mutual submission means that a wife's submission to her husband is to a man whose love and care for her is modelled on the self-sacrificing love of Jesus Christ for his Church. Any form of abuse of one's wife—verbal, emotional, or physical—is incompatible with the love of Christ, in every culture. We deny that any cultural custom or distorted biblical interpretation can justify the beating of a wife. We grieve that it is found among professing Christians, including pastors and leaders. We have no hesitation in denouncing it as a sin, and call for repentance and renunciation of it as a practice.

## Overview questions

1. Read Proverbs 3:34; 16:18–19; Isaiah 66:1–2; Philippians 2:5–11; and 1 Peter 5:5–6. What do these passages teach us about humility? Why is it beautiful in God's eyes, even though it is often seen as weakness in human eyes? How is humility expressed and perceived in your culture? Give some examples. How can we recognise pride in ourselves, and how can we resist it? Why does pride often lead to the abuse of power?

## Digging deeper

2. Why is the word "power" used so often in Scripture in relation to God and his work? Read Deuteronomy 8:11–20; Psalm 147:1–6; Luke 1:35; 4:14; Acts 1:8; Romans 1:16; 1 Corinthians 6:14; 2 Corinthians 4:7; and Revelation 19:1. How can we ensure that any power we exercise, we exercise in line with what God truly delegates to us?

3. Why is power so often abused in human relationships? In your culture, what are the practices and traditions which frequently lead to abuse of power, in relations between men and women, between employer and employee, and between political and military structures and the people? What do you think is God's judgment on such practices? How can Christians in your culture be prophetic in declaring and demonstrating what it means to "reject the idolatry of power"?

4. How does abuse of power show itself within the church? What are the special temptations to power for pastors and teachers, the wealthy, the best educated? How can a congregation or denomination safeguard against abuse of power? How do you show special care for the children and the mentally and physically vulnerable? What discipline do you introduce if a man beats his wife or an adult harms a child?

5. Why should Ephesians 5:21 and Colossians 3:5–17 never be separated from the verses which follow? What beautiful patterns are given to us for mutual relationships among God's people? How does this challenge your culture and the way your church family behaves?

## 4. Walk in integrity, rejecting the idolatry of success[110]

We cannot build the kingdom of the God of truth on foundations of dishonesty. Yet in our craving for "success" and "results" we are tempted to sacrifice our integrity, with distorted or exaggerated claims that amount to lies. Walking in the light, however, "consists in . . . righteousness and truth."[111]

---

[110] Ephesians 5:8–9.
[111] Ephesians 5:9.

*A. We call on all church and mission leaders to resist the temptation to be less than totally truthful in presenting our work.* We are dishonest when we exaggerate our reports with unsubstantiated statistics, or twist the truth for the sake of gain. We pray for a cleansing wave of honesty and the end of such distortion, manipulation, and exaggeration. We call on all who fund spiritual work not to make unrealistic demands for measurable and visible results, beyond the need for proper accountability. Let us strive for a culture of full integrity and transparency. We will choose to walk in the light and truth of God, for the Lord tests the heart and is pleased with integrity.[112]

## Overview questions

1. How would you describe integrity? Read 1 John 1:5–7 and 1 John 2:3–6, 9–11. How do these verses describe integrity in action? Why is this transparent honesty so important in God's eyes? Why is it so important for our spiritual health? Why is the temptation to seek success so powerful? How does seeking success compromise our integrity? Jesus' death seemed to many people at the time to prove that he was a failure. What can we learn from this about true success and failure?

## Digging deeper

2. In your life and ministry, what are the ways in which you are most tempted to exaggerate or bend the truth? Why are you tempted to do this? What safeguards can you put in place to live truthfully? How can we help one another own up to our failures and shortcomings? What is healthy, and what is unhealthy, about the emphasis on self-esteem found in some cultures?

---

[112] 1 Chronicles 29:17.

3. In your culture, what do people regard as success? As a Christian, what can you affirm, and what must you reject? Are there values which could be called Christian success? In what ways can we encourage a love of integrity and foster humility and generosity where there is material or other success as the world understands it?

4. What pressures do we place on mission agencies and other ministries to deliver results? What should we be looking for? Will faithful, godly ministry always produce results that can be counted (e.g., numbers of churches planted, numbers of people professing faith or being baptised)? Why? Why not? Will a faithful believer always have enough food to eat, or a faithful ministry or Bible college enough money to survive? Why? Why not? What should be our response when faced with closing down a church or ministry?

## 5. Walk in simplicity, rejecting the idolatry of greed[113]

The widespread preaching and teaching of "prosperity gospel" around the world raises significant concerns. We define prosperity gospel as the teaching that believers have a right to the blessings of health and wealth and that they can obtain these blessings through positive confessions of faith and the "sowing of seeds" through financial or material gifts. Prosperity teaching is a phenomenon that cuts across many denominations in all continents.[114]

We affirm the miraculous grace and power of God, and we welcome the growth of churches and ministries that lead people to exercise expectant faith in the living God and his supernatural power. We believe in the power of the Holy Spirit. However, we deny that God's miraculous power can be

---

[113] Ephesians 5:5.

[114] See also the full text of *The Akropong Statement: A Critique of the Prosperity Gospel Produced by African Theologians*, convened by the Lausanne Theology Working Group, at www.lausanne.org/no/documents/all/172.twg/1099-a-statement-on-the-prosperity-gospel.html.

treated as automatic, or at the disposal of human techniques, or manipulated by human words, actions, gifts, objects, or rituals.

We affirm that there is a biblical vision of human prospering, and that the Bible includes material welfare (both health and wealth) within its teaching about the blessing of God. However, we deny as unbiblical the teaching that spiritual welfare can be measured in terms of material welfare, or that wealth is always a sign of God's blessing. The Bible shows that wealth can often be obtained by oppression, deceit, or corruption. We also deny that poverty, illness, or early death are always a sign of God's curse, or evidence of lack of faith, or the result of human curses, since the Bible rejects such simplistic explanations.

We accept that it is good to exalt the power and victory of God. But we believe that the teachings of many who vigorously promote the prosperity gospel seriously distort the Bible; that their practices and lifestyle are often unethical and un-Christ-like; that they commonly replace genuine evangelism with miracle-seeking, and replace the call to repentance with the call to give money to the preacher's organization. We grieve that the impact of this teaching on many Churches is pastorally damaging and spiritually unhealthy. We gladly and strongly affirm every initiative in Christ's name that seeks to bring healing to the sick, or lasting deliverance from poverty and suffering. The prosperity gospel offers no lasting solution to poverty, and can deflect people from the true message and means of eternal salvation. For these reasons it can be soberly described as a false gospel. We therefore reject the excesses of prosperity teaching as incompatible with balanced biblical Christianity.

*A. We urgently encourage church and mission leaders* in contexts where the prosperity gospel is popular to test its teaching with careful attention to the teaching and example of Jesus Christ. Particularly, we all need to interpret and teach those Bible texts that are commonly used to support the prosperity gospel in their full biblical context and proper balance. Where prosperity teaching happens in the context of poverty, we must counter it with authentic compassion and action to bring justice and lasting transformation for the poor. Above all we must replace self-interest and greed with the biblical teaching on self-sacrifice and generous giving as the marks of true discipleship to Christ. We affirm Lausanne's historic call for simpler lifestyles.

## Overview questions

1. Read Luke 12:13–21; 19:1–10; Acts 2:44–45; 4:32–37; 5:1–11. What do these passages teach us about how we should relate to wealth and possessions? Why are generosity and sharing what we have sometimes difficult? What practical steps could we take to encourage generosity, both in what we do and among other Christian people? What does generosity *not* achieve?

## Digging deeper

2. What does "simple lifestyle" look like in your culture? Is that the way Christians are observed to live? If not, why not? What practical steps could we take to live more simply and more generously? Is it wrong to be wealthy or virtuous to be poor? What could the church do locally and globally to tackle deep causes of poverty and the ill health that often accompanies it, as well as spiritual poverty?

3. Scripture gives examples of people who trust in God being healed and people not being healed; of people being delivered from suffering and people having to endure suffering; of people prospering materially and people suffering great poverty and deprivation. Trace some of these stories in the Bible. What does it teach us about living in a fallen world, at the same time as knowing God's care and blessing? In circumstances of poverty or sickness or suffering, how should we pray?

4. Why is the gospel of grace incompatible with some forms of "prosperity gospel" teaching? What makes such teaching attractive to many people? How would you pastor someone hurt by this teaching, perhaps being told that failure to experience healing or acquire wealth must be because of personal sin or lack of faith?

5. In today's world, why is it especially important that Christian leaders should live simply and generously? What does that mean in practice in your culture? The Lord Jesus did not accumulate wealth, houses, or possessions; is it right, then, that today some Christian leaders have large houses and great wealth? What are the challenges if you live in a situation where those you lead are wealthier than you and when they are very poor? Is it ever right for a pastor or Christian worker to be wealthier than if he had stayed in his previous occupation?

# IIF

## PARTNERING IN THE BODY OF CHRIST FOR UNITY IN MISSION

Paul teaches us that Christian unity is the creation of God, based on our reconciliation with God and with one another. This double reconciliation has been accomplished through the cross. When we live in unity and work in partnership we demonstrate the supernatural, counter-cultural power of the cross. But when we demonstrate our disunity through failure to partner together, we demean our mission and message, and deny the power of the cross.

### Partnership in the gospel

The New Testament church demonstrated the power of unity as an instrument of mission. The gospel united poor and rich, beggars and academics, slave and free, men and women, Jews and Gentiles. The combined witness of their spiritual unity and economic sharing won many to faith in Jesus. At the same time, however, successful mission could pose a threat to the church's unity, whether over its social arrangements,[115] or ethnic inclusiveness,[116] or because of immaturity and factionalism (Corinth), or cultural and theological disputes (Rome). The apostles worked tirelessly to sustain the unity of the church for the sake of its witness.

Mission done in partnership can provide and demonstrate Christian unity in powerful and globally significant ways. Movements of international co-operation in mission can foster unity of purpose among local churches, reciprocal learning across boundaries of north and south, combined and effective strategic efforts, and the breaking down of old paradigms of sending and receiving countries. (For an example of partnership in mission, consider COMIBAM.)[117] At the same time, however, proliferation

---

[115] Acts 6.
[116] Acts 10–11, 15.
[117] COMIBAM [Cooperación Misionera Iberoamericana—Cooperation of Missions in Ibero-America] unites 25 countries, 400 mission agencies, and thousands

of mission initiatives can splinter the Christian community and destroy our unity.

Partnership is a journey of friendship, and is built on developing trust. Many current mission initiatives are discovering the importance of working in partnership with other churches or agencies—locally or globally. Effective partnerships will always involve personal trust building, a common vision, an agreement over strategy, transparency over finance, mutual accountability, and equality in power. Such commitments are costly. Partnerships can prevent competitive duplication, and increase potential for maximum wise deployment of resources of personnel and finance.

Since partnerships model reconciliation, humility, and refusal to build independent empires, we call upon churches and mission agencies to:

1. Develop partnerships with other likeminded groups committed to the same mission focus;

2. Send personnel to an existing ministry rather than establish a duplicate ministry;

3. Invest in the trust-building that makes partnerships possible;

Accept that different partners may bring different contributions to the whole, but refuse to allow difference of relative resources to dictate an imbalance of power.

# 1. Unity in the Church

A divided Church has no message for a divided world. Our failure to live in reconciled unity is a major obstacle to authenticity and effectiveness in mission.

A. *We lament the dividedness and divisiveness of our churches and organizations.* We deeply and urgently long for Christians to cultivate a spirit of grace and to be obedient to Paul's command to "make every effort to maintain the unity of the Spirit in the bond of peace."

B. *While we recognize that our deepest unity is spiritual, we long for greater recognition of the missional power of visible, practical, earthly unity.* So we urge Christian sisters and brothers worldwide, for the sake of our common

of churches in Latin America, the Caribbean, Hispanics in North America, and the Iberian Peninsula.

witness and mission, to resist the temptation to split the body of Christ, and to seek the paths of reconciliation and restored unity wherever possible.

## Overview questions

1. Read Psalm 133, John 17:20–23, and Ephesians 4:1–16. What do these passages teach us about how God views unity among his people? What is the effect on the unbelieving world of disunity or of unity, and why is it such a vital issue for effective mission? What is the effect on the church itself of unity or disunity? Why do we find unity so difficult to achieve? What changes do we need to make in order to be more united before the world and in the cause of the gospel?

## Digging deeper

2. Evangelicals often claim to have spiritual unity in Christ, based on their common commitment to Scripture as the Word of God. What are the strengths and weaknesses of this claim? Ecumenicals focus on outward and visible unity with others, laying greater emphasis on structural unity over and above doctrinal purity. What are the strengths and weaknesses of this aim? How can we both respect diversity and express the unity that comes from being in the one body of Christ?

3. In your local area, how do Christians of different congregations or different denominations relate to one another? How does this affect how unbelievers see the church in general? What could you do to build closer relationships and to undertake some things in the wider community together? Are the issues that divide you substantive gospel issues or differences of culture and preference? How do you discern the difference honestly? Do you have to agree on all points with others to partner with them in mission?

4. Within your own congregation, what causes broken relationships? How could you act as a peacemaker to bring about reconciliation? Why does it matter? What happens when problems are not dealt with in a godly way? Why is this a gospel issue?

## 2. Partnership in global mission

Partnership in mission is not only about efficiency. It is the strategic and practical outworking of our shared submission to Jesus Christ as Lord. Too often we have engaged in mission in ways that prioritize and preserve our own identities (ethnic, denominational, theological) and have failed to submit our passions and preferences to our one Lord and Master. The supremacy and centrality of Christ in our mission must be more than a confession of faith; it must also govern our strategy, practice, and unity.

We rejoice in the growth and strength of emerging mission movements in the majority world and the ending of the old pattern of "from the West to the Rest." But we do not accept the idea that the baton of mission responsibility has passed from one part of the world Church to another. There is no sense in rejecting the past triumphalism of the West, only to relocate the same ungodly spirit in Asia, Africa, or Latin America. No one ethnic group, nation, or continent can claim the exclusive privilege of being the ones to complete the Great Commission. Only God is sovereign.

A. *We stand together as church and mission leaders in all parts of the world,* called to recognize and accept one another, with equality of opportunities to contribute together to world mission. Let us, in submission to Christ, lay aside suspicion, competition, and pride and be willing to learn from those whom God is using, even when they are not from our continent, nor of our particular theology, nor of our organization, nor of our circle of friends.

B. *Partnership is about more than money, and unwise injection of money frequently corrupts and divides the Church.* Let us finally prove that the Church does not operate on the principle that those who have the most money have all the decision-making power. Let us no longer impose our own preferred names, slogans, programmes, systems, and methods on other parts of the Church. Let us instead work for true mutuality of North and South, East and West, for interdependence in giving and receiving, for the respect and dignity that characterizes genuine friends and true partners in mission.

## Overview questions

1. Why are there so many denominations, mission agencies, colleges and seminaries, and Christian initiatives, often working competitively in the same place? What are the advantages, and what are the problems, of such diversity? What sinful factors may have contributed to this situation? What are the positive factors? What are neutral or historical factors? What factors prevent mergers or effective partnerships in such a situation? How could you foster healthy partnerships?

## Digging deeper

2. If a group wants to begin a new ministry locally, or to develop ministry cross-culturally, or to expand into a new area, what research should they do first? What principles should determine whether or not they carry out their plans? How could they modify their plans to support an existing ministry instead? Should people follow their own vision?

3. Why is partnership in global mission so important? What does that mean in practise for your local church, or your agency? How would you set about developing partnerships that are healthy and honouring to the Lord? What are the factors that are crucial for a truly healthy partnership?

4. As the world and the world church change, how can we develop partnerships between south and north, east and west? What are the barriers? How can we overcome them? How can we live out our equality before God and share our differing gifts and history, still recognising we have different experience to contribute, different wealth of people resources or financial resources, different cultural ways of making decisions, different ways of leading? What processes or structures would facilitate trust building? Pray!

## 3. Men and women in partnership

Scripture affirms that God created men and women in his image and gave them dominion over the earth together. Sin entered human life and history through man and woman acting together in rebellion against God. Through the cross of Christ, God brought salvation, acceptance, and unity to men and women equally. At Pentecost God poured out his Spirit of prophecy on all flesh, sons and daughters alike. Women and men are thus equal in creation, in sin, in salvation, and in the Spirit.[118]

All of us, women and men, married and single, are responsible to employ God's gifts for the benefit of others, as stewards of God's grace, and for the praise and glory of Christ. All of us, therefore, are also responsible to enable all God's people to exercise all the gifts that God has given for all the areas of service to which God calls the Church.[119] We should not quench the Spirit by despising the ministry of any.[120] Further, we are determined to see ministry within the body of Christ as a gifting and responsibility in which we are called to serve, and not as a status and right that we demand.

*A. We uphold Lausanne's historic position:* "We affirm that the gifts of the Spirit are distributed to all God's people, women and men, and that their partnership in evangelization must be welcomed for the common good."[121] We acknowledge the enormous and sacrificial contribution that women have made to world mission, ministering to both men and women, from biblical times to the present.

---

[118] Genesis 1:26–28; 3; Acts 2:17–18; Galatians 3:28; 1 Peter 3:7.
[119] Romans 12:4–8; 1 Corinthians 12:4–11; Ephesians 4:7–16; 1 Peter 4:10–11.
[120] 1 Thessalonians 5:19–20; 1 Timothy 4:11–14.
[121] *The Manila Manifesto*, Affirmation 14.

*B. We recognize that there are different views sincerely held by those who seek to be faithful and obedient to Scripture.* Some interpret apostolic teaching to imply that women should not teach or preach, or that they may do so but not in sole authority over men. Others interpret the spiritual equality of women, the exercise of the edifying gift of prophecy by women in the New Testament church, and their hosting of churches in their homes, as implying that the spiritual gifts of leading and teaching may be received and exercised in ministry by both women and men.[122] We call upon those on different sides of the argument to:

1. Accept one another without condemnation in relation to matters of dispute, for while we may disagree, we have no grounds for division, destructive speaking, or ungodly hostility towards one another;[123]

2. Study Scripture carefully together, with due regard for the context and culture of the original authors and contemporary readers;

3. Recognize that where there is genuine pain we must show compassion; where there is injustice and lack of integrity we must stand against them; and where there is resistance to the manifest work of the Holy Spirit in any sister or brother we must repent;

4. Commit ourselves to a pattern of ministry, male and female, that reflects the servanthood of Jesus Christ, not worldly striving for power and status.

*C. We encourage churches to acknowledge godly women who teach and model what is good,* as Paul commanded,[124] and to open wider doors of opportunity for women in education, service, and leadership, particularly in contexts where the gospel challenges unjust cultural traditions. We long that women should not be hindered from exercising God's gifts or following God's call on their lives.

---

[122] I Timothy 2:12; 1 Corinthians 14:33–35; Titus 2:3–5; Acts 18:26; 21:9; Romans 16:1–5, 7; Philippians 4:2–3; Colossians 4:15; 1 Corinthians 11:5; 14:3–5.

[123] Romans 14:1–13.

[124] Titus 2:3–5.

## Overview questions

1.  Read Genesis 1:26–28; 3:14–19; Acts 2:17–18; and Galatians 3:28. What do these passages teach us about the equality between men and women, along with their distinctiveness, "in creation, in sin, in salvation, and in the Spirit"? How should that inform relationships between men and women in the church? What kind of partnership is being implied?

## Digging deeper

2.  Read Acts 18:24–26; Romans 16:1–3; 1 Corinthians 11:1–11; 14:33–35; and 1 Timothy 2:11–15. Why do these passages, and those under (1) above, seem to lead to confusion and some disagreements between Christians as to the place of women in the life of the church? How do you think those disagreements should be resolved? Is Paul inconsistent in his instructions and practise? If so, how do we make sense of it all? If not, how do we understand what he is saying?

3.  In your culture, what are the customary relationships between men and women? What does the Bible affirm, and what does it challenge? How can the church demonstrate healthy, respectful relationships between men and women, valuing both as God does? How can you bring up children in your culture to value Christian standards in gender relationships and ministry?

4. Whatever your understanding of the role of women in the public life of the church, how can every woman as well as every man be encouraged to use every gift God has given them for the well-being of the church and to look outwards in mission? How could you, male or female, ensure that you encourage, serve, and nurture fellow believers of both genders? Where people have been wounded within the life of the church, how can men and women work together to bring healing and reconciliation?

5. Gather stories of men and women from the past who have been used by the Lord in effective mission. Gather stories from your congregation of ways in which men and women are discipling others today. Share those stories, and then pray for everyone in their outreach, teaching, and serving.

# 4. Theological education and mission

The New Testament shows the close partnership between the work of evangelism and church planting (e.g., the Apostle Paul), and the work of nurturing churches (e.g., Timothy and Apollos). Both tasks are integrated in the Great Commission, where Jesus describes disciple-making in terms of evangelism (before "baptizing them") and "teaching them to obey all that I have commanded you." Theological education is part of mission beyond evangelism.[125]

## Two tasks

The Apostle Paul engaged in primary evangelism and church planting, but saw his overall goal as "presenting everyone mature in Christ," which required not only the task of "proclaiming" but also "teaching everyone with all wisdom."[126] His years in Ephesus included systematic daily lecturing in which he taught the churches there "the whole counsel of God." Paul worked in close partnership with those who followed up his church planting

---

[125] Colossians 1:28–29; Acts 19:8–10; 20:20, 27; 1 Corinthians 3:5–9.
[126] Colossians 1:28–29; Acts 19:8–10; 20:20, 27.

ministry with the ministry of teaching and the training of pastors, such as Timothy, Titus, and especially Apollos. But Paul saw no dichotomy between the two tasks, and no superiority of one over the other. On the contrary he insisted that his role ("planting") and Apollos's role ("watering") were both essential under God, and that the planter and the waterer "have one purpose" (literally, "they are one"). Both ministries were part of the missionary mandate and task.[127]

The mission of the Church on earth is to serve the mission of God, and the mission of theological education is to strengthen and accompany the mission of the Church. Theological education serves *first* to train those who lead the Church as pastor-teachers, equipping them to teach the truth of God's Word with faithfulness, relevance, and clarity; and *second*, to equip all God's people for the missional task of understanding and relevantly communicating God's truth in every cultural context. Theological education engages in spiritual warfare, as "we demolish arguments and every pretension that sets itself up against the knowledge of God, and we take captive every thought to make it obedient to Christ."[128]

A. *Those of us who lead churches and mission agencies need to acknowledge that theological education is intrinsically missional.* Those of us who provide theological education need to ensure that it is intentionally missional, since its place within the academy is not an end in itself, but to serve the mission of the Church in the world.

B. *Theological education stands in partnership with all forms of missional engagement.* We will encourage and support all who provide biblically-faithful theological education, formal and non-formal, at local, national, regional and international levels.

C. *We urge that institutions and programmes of theological education conduct a "missional audit"* of their curricula, structures and ethos, to ensure that they truly serve the needs and opportunities facing the Church in their cultures.

D. *We long that all church planters and theological educators should place the Bible at the centre of their partnership,* not just in doctrinal statements but in practice. Evangelists must use the Bible as the supreme source of the content and authority of their message. Theological educators must re-centre the study of the Bible as the core discipline in Christian theology,

---

[127] 1 Corinthians 3:5–9.
[128] 2 Corinthians 10:4–5.

integrating and permeating all other fields of study and application. Above all theological education must serve to equip pastor-teachers for their prime responsibility of preaching and teaching the Bible.[129]

## Overview questions

1. Read Deuteronomy 6:4–10, Psalm 119:9–16, 97–105, Matthew 28:16–20, and Acts 19:8–10. What do these passages teach us about the need for ongoing teaching and training? Who needs it? What should be our attitude to lifelong study? How do study, teaching, and daily living relate to each other? Why is deep study of the Bible so central?

## Digging deeper

2. In your church or agency, what are the different ways in which people are taught God's Word and its transforming application? In your culture, what are the most effective ways of teaching and training? Why? Do young people learn in different ways from older people? If so, why? How does your church cater for the different learning needs of different people? How do you apply this in evangelism and outreach?

3. In your culture, how are Christian leaders trained? What are the benefits and the disadvantages of full-time training in an institution? How are people selected for it? Is this form of training the best way of approaching theological education? Why? Why not? Who should be appointed to teach in academic institutions designed to train pastors and Christian leaders? What experience and qualifications should they have? What are the most vital things that should be taught?

---

[129] 2 Timothy 2:2; 4:1–2; 1 Timothy 3:2b; 4:11–14; Titus 1:9; 2:1.

4. How can theological education be "intentionally missional"? Where this is not the case, how could changes be implemented? How could churches, church planters, mission agencies, and theological educators establish better partnerships? How can places or systems of excellence in training be established in many more countries and among many more people groups?

5. In our right desire to see the unreached reached, as soon as possible, how do we also pay attention to depth and quality of discipleship? What long-term goals and strategies do pioneers need to have as people first come to faith? How can those with different gifts, and different agencies, complement one another's callings more fully? What needs to happen to bring a Christian community to maturity in Christ? What priorities should there be in establishing theological training?

# Conclusion

God was in Christ reconciling the world to himself. God's Spirit was in Cape Town, calling the Church of Christ to be ambassadors of God's reconciling love for the world. God kept the promise of his Word as his people met together in Christ's name, for the Lord Jesus Christ himself dwelt among us, and walked among us.[130]

We sought to listen to the voice of the Lord Jesus Christ. And in his mercy, through his Holy Spirit, Christ spoke to his listening people. Through the many voices of Bible exposition, plenary addresses, and group discussion, two repeated themes were heard:

▷ The need for radical obedient discipleship, leading to maturity, to growth in depth as well as growth in numbers;

▷ The need for radical cross-centred reconciliation, leading to unity, to growth in love as well as growth in faith and hope.

Discipleship and reconciliation are indispensable to our mission. We lament the scandal of our shallowness and lack of discipleship, and the scandal of our disunity and lack of love. For both seriously damage our witness to the gospel.

We discern the voice of the Lord Jesus Christ in these two challenges because they correspond to two of Christ's most emphatic words to the Church as recorded in the gospels. In Matthew's Gospel, Jesus gave us our primary mandate—to make disciples among all nations. In John's Gospel, Jesus gave us our primary method—to love one another so that the world will know we are disciples of Jesus. We should not be surprised, but rather rejoice to hear the Master's voice, when Christ says the same things 2,000 years later to his people gathered from all around the world. *Make disciples. Love one another.*

---

[130] Leviticus 26:11–12; Matthew 18:20; 28:20.

## Make disciples

Biblical mission demands that those who claim Christ's name should be like him, by taking up their cross, denying themselves, and following him in the paths of humility, love, integrity, generosity, and servanthood. To fail in discipleship and disciple-making, is to fail at the most basic level of our mission. The call of Christ to his Church comes to us afresh from the pages of the gospels: "Come and follow me"; "Go and make disciples."

## Love one another

Three times Jesus repeated, "A new command I give you: Love one another. As I have loved you, so you must love one another."[131] Three times Jesus prayed "that all of them may be one, Father."[132] Both the command and the prayer are missional. "*By this everyone will know that you are my disciples*, if you love one another." "May they be brought to complete unity *so that the world may know that you sent me*." Jesus could not have made his point more emphatically. The evangelization of the world and the recognition of Christ's deity are helped or hindered by whether or not we obey him in practice. The call of Christ and his apostles comes to us afresh: "Love one another"; "Make every effort to keep the unity of the Spirit through the bond of peace."[133] It is for the sake of God's mission that we renew our commitment to obey this "message we heard from the beginning."[134] When Christians live in the reconciled unity of love by the power of the Holy Spirit, the world will come to know Jesus, whose disciples we are, and come to know the Father who sent him.[135]

*In the name of God the Father, the Son and the Holy Spirit, and on the sole foundation of faith in God's infinite mercy and saving grace, we earnestly long and pray for a reformation of biblical discipleship and a revolution of Christ-like love.*

*We make this our prayer and we undertake this our commitment for the sake of the Lord we love and for the sake of the world we serve in his name.*

---

[131] John 13:34; 15:12; 17.
[132] John 17:21–23.
[133] Ephesians 4:1–6; Colossians 3:12–14; 1 Thessalonians 4:9–10; 1 Peter 1:22; 1 John 3:11–14; 4:7–21.
[134] 1 John 3:11.
[135] In October 2011, minor changes were made to Sections IIA6 and IIC5. These changes are reflected in *The Cape Town Commitment: Study Edition*.

## Final Overview questions

1. Which parts of the CTC have been most challenging to you? Why?

2. What priorities will you set in response?

3. How will you put into practice the commitments you have made?

"May the Lord bless you and keep you, growing in likeness to our Saviour, and effective in his service, all your life long. Grace and peace."